937.02

Henri Stierlin

PHOTOGRAPHS: ANNE AND HENRI STIERLIN

THE ROMAN EMPIRE

VOLUME 1   FROM THE ETRUSCANS TO
            THE DECLINE OF THE ROMAN EMPIRE

TASCHEN

KÖLN LISBOA LONDON NEW YORK PARIS TOKYO

Page 3
The great plan of Rome, known as the
forma urbis (18 by 13 meters) created
during the reign of Septimius Severus,
between A.D. 203 and 211, was
engraved on a slab of marble in the
library of the Temple of Peace in the
forum built by Vespasian. This fragment which shows the theater of
Pompey, built circa 50 B.C., indicates
that Roman plans respected the same
conventions that modern plans do.

Page 5
Gold coin portrait of Octavian-
Augustus, circa 27 B.C.
(Museo Nazionale Romano, Rome)

This book was printed on 100% chlorine-free bleached paper
in accordance with the TCF standard.

© 1996 Benedikt Taschen Verlag GmbH
Hohenzollernring 53, D-50672 Köln

Edited by Silvia Kinkel, Cologne
Design and layout: Marion Hauff, Milan
Cover design: Marion Hauff, Milan; Angelika Muthesius, Cologne
English translation: Suzanne Bosman, London

Printed in Italy
ISBN 3-8228-8562-2

Contents

INTRODUCTION

The Genius of Rome

The architecture that the Romans created is one of the most significant in human history. For centuries, from the time of the Etruscans and the Republic to the end of the Empire on the eve of the barbarian invasions, the Romans created a wealth of major buildings. They revolutionized building techniques, with their repeated use of the arch, the vault, and the dome. They designed grandiose and imaginative spatial schemes.

The buildings that survive today, broadly dating from the end of the second century B.C. to the beginning of the fourth century A.D., demonstrate the Roman genius for architecture. Often the structures are so well preserved that the observer can judge the technological progress made during that time and develop an understanding of the underlying motivation of those who built them.

This book provides an understanding of how Roman architecture, whether in the form of sanctuaries, palaces, baths, markets, private homes, aqueducts, or tombs, differs from that of classical Greece and the Hellenistic period, of which it is in part the direct heir. It also defines the spatial discoveries and technological innovations that the Roman spirit brought to the conception and realization of sacred and civic monuments.

The Differences between Roman and Greek Architecture

The study of architecture requires an examination of the mentality, the religious beliefs, and the driving force of a whole civilization. In order to understand the essential character of Roman architecture, for example, it is not enough to know, according to Vitruvius's treatises, that the Romans used the three great classical orders: Doric, Ionic, and Corinthian. Rather, the originality of Roman builders lies less in their decorative and ornamental schemes than in the creation of spatial relationships, curvilinear forms, vaults supported by arcades, and vast domed structures covering large halls, intended as much for civic use as for the pomp of religious ceremonies or of the imperial court.

Unlike the Greek temple, essentially a structure for the play of light and shade, with little interior space accommodating a small sanctuary, Roman builders typically used arches, vaults, matching domes, or sweeping areas of concrete to cover huge spaces.

The Greeks used the static *trilithon* design: two pillars or columns supporting an architrave — in effect, a pair of vertical supports linked by a horizontal lintel, which absorbed the stresses of the building. The Romans, on the other hand, employed a dynamic structure based on elements deployed in a succession of circular load-bearing arcs to cope with the tensions that ran through the entire construction.

The architectural vocabulary of the two traditions is very different as well. That the Romans built temples with peristyles and saddlebacked roofs based on the Greek model is true. However, the vault was unknown in classical Greek architecture and starts to appear only at the beginning of the Hellenistic period. And although the Greeks created semicircular tiers of seating for their theaters set into the flanks of hills excavated for this purpose, the technique of using arches as a way of creating the *cavea*'s substructure remained unknown to them. However, the *tholos*, or round temple, was already evolving during the classical period.

In addition, the skill of Roman architects in their development of the arch and the ever-increasing load-bearing vault in the form of relatively thin layers of concrete found perfect expression in thermal baths, *nymphaea*, places of worship, and palaces dedicated to court rituals. In a similar way, the ingenuity of engineers, from the end of the Hellenistic period onward, resulted in the construction of sophisticated hydraulic systems such as aqueducts, prompting Frontinus to admire their functionality, when he contrasted them to the pyramids of Egypt, "which obviously serve no useful purpose" (*De aquis urbis Romae*, 16).

The Differences between East and West

This architectural heritage covering four centuries is indeed considerable and so rich that it would be impossible to treat the output of the Latin-speaking world in the West together with that of the vast reaches of the eastern Mediterranean where Greek was the *lingua franca*, despite the might of Imperial Rome.

To understand the importance of the architecture of the West, it is necessary to analyze different types of buildings and also to follow their development down the centuries – over half a millennium – throughout the Roman world. Beyond Italy, this huge area included Gaul, Spain, Portugal, the Rhineland, Great Britain, as well as North Africa, from Morocco to the Tripolitanian province in Libya, including Algeria and Tunisia. The breadth of this field of research is huge, and the number of buildings that survive is so extensive that it would be impractical for the purposes of this book to compile a comprehensive list.

By limiting this study to the provinces that made up the western Roman empire, the whole of the Greek-speaking empire – a huge area beyond the Adriatic, including Greece, Asia Minor, Mesopotamia to the Persian Gulf, the borders of Arabia, as well as Alexandria and Cyrenaica – is excluded. When compared to the western empire, the East forms a separate cultural identity, with its own style of architecture. Consequently, the monuments belonging to the Greek-speaking empire, from the Balkans to the Euphrates, will be examined in a second volume concentrating on the Graeco-Roman Orient.

This separation, dictated by the striking architectural and semiological differences of each region, reflects the division that occurred with successive splits in the late period. The schisms that separated the western and eastern empire always followed linguistic frontiers.

Surviving Monuments

The subject matter of any architectural study of the Roman world is greatly dependent on the works that have survived – essentially those monuments that survived the ravages of the Middle Ages and the destruction that has occurred since the Renaissance. Consequently only buildings that are sufficiently well preserved will be discussed to describe the history of the builders of the Roman world and present a picture of the Roman architectural ideal.

The fundamental ingredient in architecture is the perception of space, and the basic condition for understanding spatial relationships is the state in which the buildings in question survive. This book therefore gives priority to buildings that are more or less intact or have been restored by archaeologists, enabling us to understand the intentions of the ancient architects.

Map of the Roman Empire
at the beginning of the second century A.D.

- • Cities and towns
- —·—·—· Frontiers of the empire under Trajan
- ---------- Frontiers of the provinces
- |||||||||| Walls (limes)
- ·········· Linguistic boundaries

0 100 200 300 400 500 1000 1500 2000 KM

0 100 200 300 400 500 1000 1500 MILES

Hadrian's Wall

BRITAIN

Silchester

GAUL

Cologne

BELGIUM

Trier (Treverorum)

Rhine Wall

GERMANY

Rhine

Rheims (Durocortorum)

LUGDUNENSIS

RAETIA

NORICUM

Danube Wall

DACIA

AQUITANIA

Lyon (Lugdunum)

Vienne

Aosta (Augusta Praetoria)

Aquileia

PANNONIA

Danube

Rhône

NARBONENSIS

Milan

Nîmes (Nemausus)

Orange (Arausio)

Arles (Arelate)

Saint-Rémy (Glanum)

Narbonne (Narbo)

Marseille (Massilia)

ITALY

DALMATIA

Split (Spalato)

MOESIA

Tarragona

CORSICA

ADRIATIC SEA

THRACE

Tivoli
Rome
Ostia Castel Gandolfo

Hadrianopolis

MACEDONIA

Salonica (Thessalonike)

Pydna

Cyzicus

Anzio (Antium)
Sperlonga

Capua
Naples

SARDINIA

TYRRHENIAN SEA

Pergamon

ASIA

Cagliari

GREECE

AEGEAN SEA

IONIAN SEA

Nicopolis
Actium
Cynocephal
Delphi

Eleusis

Ephesus
Magnesia

Laodicea ad Lycum

MAURITANIA

SICILY

Piazza Armerina

Corinth
Olympia

Athens

Didyma

Alabandes
Halicarnassus

Delos

Carthage

Djemila (Cuicul)

Zaghouan

Dougga (Thugga)

Rhodes

NUMIDIA

Lambaesis

Timgad (Thamugadi)

El Djem (Thysdrus)

CRETE

TUNISIA

MEDITERRANEAN SEA

Sabratha

Leptis Magna

Cyrene

LIBYA

PROCONSULAR AFRICA

CYRENAICA

EGYPT

Prologue

The birth of Roman architecture owes much to the various influences that the Romans absorbed; initially much indebted to the Italic tribes and the Etruscans, artistic creation derived primarily from the legacy of the achievements of the Hellenistic age, which proved fertile terrain for the evolution of Roman architectural thought, thanks to the profound achievements wrought by the Greeks through their close links with the Orient. Until the end of the Republican era, these influences were decisive. But Rome soon penetrated Asia and drew directly from Asian sources. This was especially the case during the campaigns of Sulla in Cilicia and Greece in 92–85 B.C. Grandiose structures such as the temple of Fortuna Primigenia at Praeneste and the temple of Jupiter Anxur at Terracina owe their existence to these campaigns.

When Caesar developed the heart of Rome with the construction of the Forum, the pattern was established. Later, when Augustus took power and the Imperial Age began, the style of architecture spread throughout the territories occupied by Roman legions. Developments in Gaul, in particular, closely mirrored those of Rome. Grand town planning projects – forum, capitol, temple, cultural and sporting arenas – were initiated. The influence of Rome was reflected everywhere in the planning and creation of towns, with replicas, in miniature, of the center of imperial power. In Gaul, as throughout the rest of the Empire, the Romans undertook major land improvements started during the Republic. They created roads that had both commercial and strategic importance, and built bridges, aqueducts and reservoirs.

The true expression of the Roman spirit in architecture, hampered for a period by Augustus's restraint and the reactionary attitude of Vitruvius (the first Roman theoretician on the art of building), became clear to see from the high Imperial Age, from Tiberius to Nero and Domitian. The style that flourished during that period was characterized by the creation of huge interior spaces, intended as much for religious purposes as for the pomp and splendor of the palaces, baths, and amphitheaters that exalted the power of empire in Rome and in the western provinces.

In A.D. 79, however, during the thriving dynasty of the Flavians, a catastrophe struck the pleasure domes of Roman society: the eruption of Vesuvius destroyed Pompeii, Herculaneum, Stabia, and Oplontis. This event, which killed large numbers of people and plunged Rome into shock, has been a blessing for archaeologists and historians, for it left these towns suspended in time at the end of the first century A.D. Excavations have revealed the daily lives of well-to-do families in the environs of Naples, untouched by any alteration. These discoveries have illuminated our understanding not only of those urban systems and the character of the bourgeois household, but also the character of their architecture, represented in paintings and decoration.

At the dawn of the second century A.D., imperial art reached its zenith with the grandiose creations of Trajan and Hadrian. Two projects particularly illustrate their breadth of vision: on the one hand, the Forum of Trajan built by Apollodorus in the new heart of the capital and, on the other, port cities such as Ostia. But the period of the Antonine dynasty was equally productive throughout the empire. Particular opulence was showered on Spain when Trajan and Hadrian, both of Spanish origin, were emperors. This richness also reflected on the whole of the West, where new cults emerged, such as that of Mithras, the oriental sun god who was venerated by Nero. Many of the cult's sanctuaries have survived almost intact.

It was during Hadrian's peaceful reign that Roman architecture reached its climax. The Pantheon of Rome and Hadrian's villa at Tivoli bear eloquent testimony to the potential of curvilinear solutions. At that time buildings assumed a rich

Pages 8/9
Map of the Roman Empire
The Latin-speaking area is bounded to the east by the *limes* of the Rhine and the eastern coast of the Adriatic. On the African coast, it stretches across to Tripolitania, excluding Cyrenaica, which was under Greek influence.

A reminiscence of Roman splendor

The modern reconstruction of the Roman villa built for the Paul Getty Foundation in Malibu is a reconstruction of the Villa dei Papiri, or Villa of the Pisones, at Herculaneum. The garden, surrounded by porticoes, is adorned by a huge central pool. Such was the setting of the sumptuous lifestyle enjoyed by prosperous Romans during Augustus's reign.

semiological meaning. It is the deciphering of this symbolic meaning that constitutes one of the major achievements of the modern approach to the history of architecture.

On Septimius Severus's accession, a person of North African origin ruled the ancient world. Not only did the provinces to the south of the Mediterranean, Algeria, Tunisia, and Tripolitania, enjoy a rich prosperity reflected in the sumptuousness of their architecture, but the period also marked the birth of an innovative "baroque" style.

From the time of Aurelius, who restored the stability of the Empire after the barbarian offensives, Roman building asserted itself more than ever by sheer size. The baths of Diocletian, the Aula Palatina at Trier, and the basilica of Maxentius, in Rome, stand as witness to this movement — the swan song of Rome, before the collapse of the Empire and invasions from the East.

This is the outline that will be followed in this account of the principal monuments that Roman civilization bequeathed. Rome's architecture, perhaps its highest achievement, has been its legacy, passed on to us through the architecture of the Romanesque period, the Renaissance, the Baroque and Neoclassicism and still influencing us today. This legacy attests to the grandeur and influence of Roman genius.

MASTERPIECES OF THE REPUBLIC

The Origins of Roman Architecture

Many people believe that Roman architecture evolved wholly from that which flourished in Greece during the classical and Hellenistic periods. Though it is true that in many respects the Roman world stems from Greek influence, Rome evolved in a unique historical environment and in the center of Italy, where Greek colonization had never become firmly established. For in the eighth and seventh centuries B.C., the cities of Magna Graeca in southern Italy and Sicily met with fierce resistance north of Cumae on the part of the Samnite and Volsci tribes, as well as with the increasing power of the Etruscans.

The Sources of the Art of Building

In reality a number of influences contributed to the blossoming of Roman civilization. Amongt these, the originality of native elements must be stressed. The characteristics derived from prehistoric Italic tribes soon combined with outside influences from the Hellenic colonies, mainland Greece and its islands, and Asia Minor.

In the Iron Age from the tenth century B.C. onward, the Villanovan culture (the name derives from the site of Villanova di Castenaso in the Po valley) already enjoyed a certain prosperity due to the mineral resources of Etruria. Hut-shaped funeral urns found in Villanovan tombs give an indication of the appearance of the primitive dwelling. Round in form, it possessed a single square doorway and was covered by a ridge backed roof with protruding ridge-beams. Openings in the roof let out the smoke from the hearth.

Etruscan civilization, once thought to be from Asia Minor, is now thought to be a native civilization with a strong Greek influence due to trading links with Greece and the markets of southern Italy and Sicily. New imported elements grafted themselves onto the old Villanovan base: red and black pottery from Corinth and Attica (sixth to fifth centuries B.C.), soon to be produced locally by Greek artists who settled around Veii and Tarquinia, and then imitated by Etruscan potters; painting inherited from Greek cities (Paestum); bronze work that soon reached a high degree of competence; large-scale sculpture in terracotta in the style of Ionic statuary; temple structure and decoration inspired by the Greek sanctuaries, as well as rectilinear town plans (fourth century B.C.) evoking the ideas formulated by Hippodamus of Miletus (as displayed at Spina).

The Etruscan sanctuary with its columns of wood or tufa (volcanic rock), its entablature of wood, its facade covered in terracotta ornament, frieze, acroterion and antefix, and its *cella* greater in width than in depth (an oblong format) is only partly modelled along Greek lines. Squat and placed on a podium, it anticipates the first primitive Roman temples. Statues of the gods stood on top of its ridge-backed roof. Later the style grew closer to the Greek model, absorbing the influence of Hellenistic art, as terracotta models found in tombs illustrate.

Etruscan funerary practices created different types of tomb, built or hewn out of tufa. At Cerveteri, for example, there are circular tombs whose shape is reminiscent of prehistoric tumuli from the Bronze Age. They contained one or several underground burial chambers covered by a mass of earth in the form of a hillock. The entrance was a short corridor (*dromos*) with a corbelled vault. The rock inside was sculpted to give the appearance of an Etruscan dwelling. The format was rectangular, with a ridge-backed roof and details of its wooden structure scrupulously reproduced in stone. In the main chamber, the funerary beds were arranged in a way that anticipated the Roman *triclinium*, which was to become one of the essential elements of the patrician household.

There is also another type of burial system at Cerveteri, arranged by streets on a grid pattern dividing the tombs into blocks (an early form of *insulae*), each containing several family tombs. Each block had a low facade, which could be many meters long. These blocks were built with regular dressed stone, plain in style (or sometimes carved directly out of the rock). The layout of these tombs reflects the rectilinear town planning of actual cities, such as Marzabotto.

The third type of Etruscan tomb was hollowed out of a cliff face or the ground, hidden to the outside. The painted underground hypogea of Tarquinia and the cave tombs with chambers cut into the rocky hills of the Tuscan countryside (at Vulci and Chiusi) belong to this category.

The interior of the tombs, a succession of chambers, lobbies, and annexes, reveals an important development of the private dwelling. The doors and windows, slightly trapezoidal in shape, pillars and columns, and alcoves and niches all provide an indication of the nature of everyday Etruscan architecture. There are virtually no remains of actual Etruscan homes.

Page 17
Etruscan tombs
Some of the Etruscan tombs in the Cerveteri necropolis are built out of handsome blocks of tufa and follow an orthogonal plan. They comprise sloping walls that line rectilinear streets, reflecting the planning of towns.

In the city of the dead
Etruscan tumulus in the necropolis of Cerveteri (seventh to fourth centuries B.C.). On a circular base carved out of tufa, within which the funerary chamber was hollowed out, the earth hillock is covered with vegetation, complying with a formula that would continue with the large imperial mausoleums of Rome (Augustus, Hadrian).

Vaulted entrance of an Etruscan burial mound in Cerveteri
The construction in large slabs of stone follows the technique of a corbelled vault with rows of slightly overlapping horizontal blocks. The true vault with arch-stones does not appear in Roman architecture until the fourth century B.C.

Sarcophagi in an Etruscan tomb
Carved out of tufa, the Etruscan tomb covered by the tumulus displays an internal arrangement that imitates the characteristics of the homes of the living. Consisting of a ridge-backed roof (with two slopes) and central beam, it forms a space where the sarcophagi are disposed like the couches of a *triclinium*.

Antichamber of a rock tomb
Inside an Etruscan chambered tomb at Cerveteri, the spatial organization consists of a vestibule that precedes the funerary chamber itself. Between these two rooms with ceilings like the beamed roofs of the urban home, are doors and windows that are often trapezoidal in shape.

The Archaic Legacy

The Etruscans were not the only people to influence the origins of Rome. In the fifth and fourth centuries B.C., the Latins were at war with their neighbors, the Volsci and the Samnites. The Volsci built powerful acropolises with mighty walls built out of polygonal, often cyclopean, blocks of stone, as at Alatri and Norba. These formidable fortifications did not, however, succeed in keeping the Romans at bay. This military architecture on such a grand scale, using construction techniques undoubtedly derived from the Greeks, serves as a model for the first Roman cities.

This is particularly true of Cosa (Ansedonia), a fortress town founded by Rome in 273 B.C. to guard the port of Orbetello and Monte Argentario, famous for its mines during the height of Etruscan influence. Overlooking the sea, its powerful fortifications protected a city complete with forum and acropolis built in a regular grid pattern. The *comitum* where the *comites* (or counselors) met was a circular area surrounded by raised seating, as at Paestum.

The First Roman Temples

The few buildings surviving from the Republic generally bore the stamp of the Hellenistic style that developed in Greece and in the Near East from the third to the first century B.C. as a result of Alexander's victorious campaigns in Asia. This influence also came to the fore in Rome as a result of several major historical events: the capture in 212 of Syracuse and then of Capua and Tarento, Greek cities in close contact with Alexandria; then the direct contact with the East as a result of the military campaigns — the Roman invasion of Macedonia in 199 B.C., the victory of Lucius Cornelius Scipio Asiaticus over Antiochus III in 190 B.C., the will of Attalus III, bequeathing the kingdom of Pergamon to the Romans in 133 B.C., followed by the creation of the province of Asia in 130 B.C., and Sulla's campaigns between 92 and 85 B.C. in Cilicia, Greece and Asia against Mithridates VI, king of Pontus.

In the middle of the second century B.C., the Greek architect Hermodorus of Salamina was commissioned to build two hexastyle marble temples in Rome — one dedicated to Jupiter and the other to Juno. Little of them remains today. By the Largo Argentina in Rome, the *area sacra*, uncovered by excavations in 1930, revealed the foundations of four temples built in a row, dating from the third and

second centuries B.C. The foundations of a *tholos* flanked by two sanctuaries with peristyles show that the round sanctuary existed very early on. These buildings were constructed on a podium, a formula that is one of the enduring characteristics of the Roman temple. The group, built in tufa, displays the juxtaposition of religious buildings that was common in the Greek world.

The only temples of Rome dating from the second and first centuries B.C. that are well preserved are the two sanctuaries of the Forum Boarium (Forum of the Oxen). One, dedicated to Portunus (the tutelary divinity of the port on the Tiber nearby), was also known as the Fortuna Virilis. It was a small tetrastyle building on a podium reached by a central stairway. The facade was made up of two rows of four tufa columns and a pediment. Behind these fluted Ionic shafts, the *cella* was surrounded by engaged columns.

The neighboring sanctuary, dedicated to Hercules Victor, and dating from the end of the second century B.C., was in the form of a *tholos*. Its elegant Corinthian columns were made from Pentelic marble that Greek quarrymen must have transported to Rome and finished work on *in situ*. This round temple, now without its entablature and its original roof, stands on circular steps, in accordance with the Greek formula.

Dating from 100 B.C., the temple of Cori, situated 50 kilometers southeast of Rome, was also dedicated to Hercules. From its dominant position, the lofty outline of this Republican building, perched high on its podium, dominates the agrarian landscape. Its tetrastyle facade of finely fluted columns with elongated Doric capitals was somewhat austere in style. A frieze of triglyphs punctuated its entablature beneath the pediment, now devoid of its sculpture. In the city of Tivoli

The fortified city of Norba
The impressive cyclopean fortifications of Norba (fourth century B.C.) have a projecting rounded postern, that protects the entrance to the Volsci's lofty town, perched in the foothills of the Lepini Mountains to the southeast of Rome.

Map of central Italy illustrating the principal sites mentioned in the text
This area where the Italic tribes – Etruscans, Volsci, Sabines, Samnites, and Latins – struggled for domination became the cradle of Roman power that later dominated the Mediterranean basin.

(Tibur) to the east of Rome, the *tholos* known as the temple of the Sibyl or of the goddess Vesta, dating from 72 B.C., is a circular sanctuary in the Corinthian style. Its 18 columns stand on a podium, which in turn stands on an artificial terrace built into the slope of the site, dominating the surrounding area, as at Cori. The cylindrical tufa *cella* was ornamented with bays framed in marble.

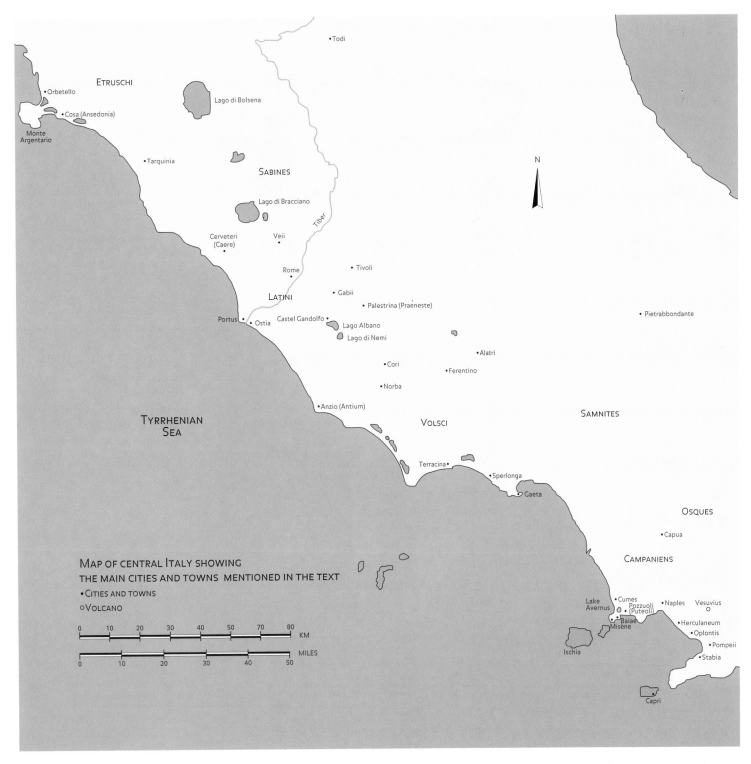

• Todi

ETRUSCHI

• Orbetello

Lago di Bolsena

• Cosa (Ansedonia)

Monte Argentario

• Tarquinia

SABINES

Lago di Bracciano

Cerveteri (Caere)

Veii

Tiber

• Tivoli

Rome

• Gabii

LATINI

• Palestrina (Praeneste)

• Pietrabbondante

Portus • Ostia

Castel Gandolfo •

Lago Albano

Lago di Nemi

• Alatri

• Cori

• Ferentino

• Norba

• Anzio (Antium)

SAMNITES

TYRRHENIAN SEA

VOLSCI

Terracina •

• Sperlonga

Gaeta

OSQUES

• Capua

MAP OF CENTRAL ITALY SHOWING
THE MAIN CITIES AND TOWNS MENTIONED IN THE TEXT
• CITIES AND TOWNS
○ VOLCANO

CAMPANIENS

Lake Avernus

• Cumes
Pozzuoli (Puteoli)

• Naples

Vesuvius ○

Baiae
Misène

• Herculaneum

• Oplontis

Ischia

• Pompeii

• Stabia

0	10	20	30	40	50	70	80

KM

MILES

0	10	20	30	40	50

Capri

Sulla and the Signs of Monarchy

In 92 B.C., Lucius Cornelius Sulla (138–78 B.C.) was nominated governor of Cilicia in the southeast of Anatolia, now under Roman domination. He nominated Ariobarzanus king of Cappadocia. A Chaldaean astrologer told him that he would have a brillant future.

On the Euphrates, Sulla negotiated with the envoy of the Parthian king, Arsaces VIII, ruler over Persia and Mesopotamia. Thereafter, the strength of the Parthians (and then the Sassanids) would be the main adversary of Rome until the intervention of the Arabs in the seventh century A.D.

During the Samnite war, Sulla conquered the last rebel Italic tribe, a triumph that made him consul in 88 B.C. He then led the campaign against Mithridates VI, king of Pontus (north of Asia Minor, on the Black Sea). In 86–85, he attacked Mithridates at Epirus, captured and pillaged Athens, despoiled the temples of Delphi and Olympia, and obtained victory at Cheronea and then at Orchomenon.

His military success was such that he had himself named *Epaphrodite*, "beloved of Aphrodite" (or Venus). He then took the title *imperator*.

But the people deprived him of his triumphs by entrusting their leadership to Marius. Sulla thus declared Marius to be a public enemy and marched on Rome. In 83/82 B.C., a brutal civil war caused terrible destruction, and the town of Praeneste was pillaged. Sulla was victorious once again and in 81 B.C. obtained the dictatorship for life with the title of *Felix*. He was considered the gods' favorite. It was said that if he was crowned by success and beloved of good fortune, he must be of divine blood and could adorn himself with the symbols of divine rulers, a characteristic typical of Hellenistic kings. However, in 79 B.C., aware that he could not succeed in imposing his monarchical views on Rome, he resigned, abandoning the dictatorship. He died less than a year later.

Temple to Fortuna Virilis
In Rome's Forum Boarium, the temple known as Fortuna Virilis is dedicated to Portunus, tutelar divinity of the port on the nearby Tiber. Built in approximately 100 B.C., the temple is a tetrastyle on a podium reached by a flight of steps. Its fluted columns, with Ionic bases and capitals, are free-standing along the front and embedded along the *cella*.

The Rise of Vaulted Construction

As the religious architecture of small Republican sanctuaries was evolving, major improvements were also being made in the techniques used in major civic projects. Indeed, it was for utilitarian buildings, such as warehouses and depots, that vaulting was first employed. In 179 B.C., the Porticus Aemilia built by the Tiber was a huge covered area, with pillars supporting no less than 200 barrel vaults. It was not long before the apsidal vault began to appear in this type of building.

The most important construction of Republican Rome is the Tabularium, built in the time of Sulla. Traces of it remain at the edge of the Forum. Built against the Capitoline hill, this huge edifice was intended to house the state archives and the treasury. The lower level had a row of small windows running the length of its 70 meters. On the first floor, the portico, built by 78 B.C. consisted of vaulted arcades resting on solid pillars decorated with embedded Doric columns.

Thereafter, the principle of arcades and vaults, a main characteristic of Roman architecture, continued to evolve. It was applied equally to basilicas (Basilica Aemilia and then later Basilica Julia) and dockside warehouses, and was also used in the construction of the huge basements beneath sanctuaries and palaces. This technical advance, introducing structures of great solidity and permitting the solid roofing of vast areas, involved a widespread application of both the voussoired arch (already used in aqueducts), which was frequently used to intersect arcades, and also of the vault. The latter was usually created by means of a type of concrete composed of mortar made of *pozzolana* (volcanic dust from Pozzuoli near Naples), mixed with gravel, tufa, and pulverized brick.

Great Sanctuaries of Hellenistic Inspiration

From Sulla's dictatorship (138–78 B.C.), Roman architecture expanded on a grand scale, inspired by the vast complexes built in the Hellenistic period, including the sanctuaries of Lindos and Cos and the acropolis at Pergamon. With the temple of Fortuna at Praeneste (modern-day Palestrina), the sanctuary of Hercules Victor at Tibur (modern-day Tivoli), and the temple of Jupiter Anxur at Terracina, architecture flourished and assumed such proportions that it amounted to a total reorganization of the landscape.

Paradoxically, the sanctuary of Fortuna at Praeneste, 30 kilometers east of Rome, displays a Hellenistic influence, while simultaneously vigorously asserting

Sanctuary of Hercules
Dominating the valley, the Doric temple of Cori, built around 100 B.C., is a tetrastyle with fluted columns with a base (contrary to Greek Doric) and a capital whose echinus is narrow and elongated. The slender architrave supports a frieze of triglyphs.

Marble temple in the Forum Boarium
Built at the end of the second century B.C., the *tholos* (round temple) of the Forum Boarium in Rome was dedicated to Hercules Victor. Its Corinthian columns surrounding a cylindrical *cella* supported an architrave and roof that have disappeared.

the originality of Roman architecture. The huge edifice was built on the flank of a hill where the slope was entirely remodeled over a width of 200 meters to a height of almost 100 meters. With the acropolis of the temple of Athena at Lindos (end of the fourth century B.C.) as its inspiration, this design marked the mastery of the builder over nature.

On a steep slope facing south, the construction consisted of a series of terraces and ramps, stretching over six levels, starting from the forum of the city whose origins date back to an early Etruscan period. Today, the layout set down during the Republican era still governs the spatial arrangement of the medieval and Renaissance town in modern-day Palestrina. Additional buildings, however, have partially obscured the original design. Recourse to a description of the archaeological ruins, which are substantial, is necessary in order to understand the grandiose design of the sanctuary dedicated to Fortuna Primigenia.

At the foot of the steep hill, on a level with the ancient forum, a two-storied portico set against a powerful buttressing wall formed a transversal basilica, flanked on one side by a building designed as a treasury and on the other by an apse in the form of a nymphaeum containing an oracular grotto with a magnificent mosaic floor.

The link between this lower level and the upper terraces was made from the sides of the construction. Above a first narrow platform, the second terrace was reached by stairways from which two ramps converged symmetrically toward a central landing. Closed off from the exterior by walls that hid the view over the

Corinthian style at Tivoli
At Tivoli (Tibur), close to Rome, stands the *tholos* of the building known as the sanctuary of the Sibyl or Vesta. It is a Corinthian-style edifice that was built during Sulla's dictatorship, around 80 B.C. The refinement and elegance of its capitals is matched by its frieze of garlands alternating with bulls' heads.

valley, these covered inclines must have been plunged in gloomy darkness. The pilgrim then emerged into full sunlight on the third level, where he could take in the surrounding view. The process was, in effect, a journey of initiation.

Ionic-columned porticoes ran along the whole length of the third level. In the middle of each of the two wings was a semicircular *exedra* with coffered barrel vaults, a daring innovation made possible through the use of concrete, destined for a glorious future in imperial art.

Sacrificial altars stood in the recesses formed by these *exedras*. In the centre of the portico, an axial staircase gave access to the fourth very narrow level, along which ran a supporting wall with large stonework recesses intended to increase its buttressing role. A second flight of central stairs led to a large, irregular oblong piazza that dominated the whole composition. This high terrace was surrounded on three sides by porticoes, formed by a double row of columns that enclosed the large open space, which seemed almost as if suspended between heaven and earth. From this fifth level overlooking the valley, another central staircase led to a remarkable structure: the *cavea* of a theater oriented toward the valley, crowned with a semicircular double-colonnaded ambulatory. Behind this curvilinear portico, and almost hidden by it, stood the *tholos*, forming the holy of holies of the sanctuary. Here, as if beneath a celestial canopy, stood the statue of the goddess Fortuna, under whose protection Sulla had placed himself. Haunted by the desire to assume royal power, the omnipotent dictator, creator of this fabulous decor, hoped to gain favor with Tyche, the Greek goddess of fortune. The site is outstanding in many respects: the stunning impact of the sanctuary, which totally transforms the hill; the breadth of a complex more geographical than architectural

Exedra of the temple of Fortuna at Praeneste
The sanctuary of Praeneste (Palestrina), dedicated to Fortuna Primigenia, was built (or restored) in Sulla's time (circa 80 B.C.). He constructed the vast terraces and ramps over 200 meters in width on the flank of the hill. On the third level stand two semicircular *exedras* flanked by Ionic-columned porticoes.

Concrete vaulting

The eastern *exedra* of Praeneste possesses a circular coffered vault achieved by molded concrete. This solid roof-covering rests on a concrete retaining wall with a reticulated covering on the side abutting the hill and, at the front, on Ionic columns arranged in a semicircle on the other side.

Axonometric view of the sanctuary at Praeneste

The temple of Fortuna at Praeneste, according to an axonometric drawing that reconstructs the original appearance of the whole scheme built on the flank of the hill. Above the basilical hall and *nymphaeum*, terraces and ramps converge toward the central flights of stairs. The third level, with its two exedras, precedes a rectangular esplanade surrounded on three sides by porticoes. At the summit, a theater *cavea* supports a double-porticoed ambulatory standing in front of the *tholos* of the goddess Fortuna which constitutes the sanctuary's holy of holies.

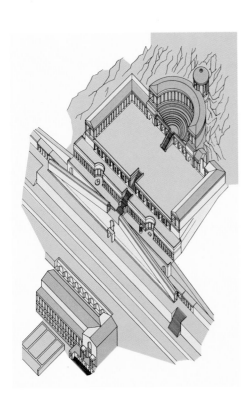

in character; the phenomenal virtuosity of the organization of space and the itinerary for visitors. But above all, the close ritual association between the theater and the holy of holies should be stressed, forming an illustration of the Birth of Tragedy with its Nietzschean juxtaposition of chthonian rites (the grotto) and celestial worship (crowning *tholos*).

A similar architectural configuration exists in the temple of Hercules at Tivoli. But before leaving this exceptional temple of Fortuna at Praeneste, it is important to stress the influence that this "royalist" work, created during the Republican period, would have on the future of imperial architecture and to note how it differed significantly from similar creations of the Hellenistic age. Indeed, a comparison with the sanctuary of Athena at Lindos or the Asklepeion on the island of Cos (both built between the end of the fourth and the beginning of the second century B.C.) reveals a similar succession of superimposed terraces with oblong courtyards and esplanades linked by stairways. There, as here, the height variations, the porticoes doubling back on themselves, and the dominant position of the holy of holies surrounded by colonnades at the highest point of the ensemble were all handled with virtuosity.

The Roman contribution at Praeneste was the introduction of a new architectural vocabulary: semicircular *exedras* with barrel-vaulted porticoes, supporting walls with cul-de-four niches, a general use of curvilinear and circular forms, the integration of a *tholos* and a *cavea* crowned with its semicircular ambulatory, all contained within a grand plan based on a strict symmetrical and axial organization. All this is evidence of a global vision and a unified scheme, that is repeated at Tivoli, "the model of Roman architecture *par excellence*", according to Bernard Andreae.

Ionic shaft of the exedral porticoes
The base of a fluted Ionic column from the sanctuary at Praeneste. The profile of the molding's design shows similarities with the "Attic base," as described by Vitruvius.

The sanctuary of Hercules Victor at Tivoli was also built during Sulla's dictatorship in 80 B.C. As at Palestrina, it stands on a hill, and this dominant position obliged the architect to construct a huge artificial terrace in order to erect the temple proper. He established huge foundations on the sloping terrain by building solid three-story porticoes with concrete vaulting. Perpendicular arcades buttressed a large underground barrel-vaulted nave. The temple of Jupiter Anxur at Terracina overlooking the sea near Gaeta was built on the same principle. Embedded Doric columns made of stonework punctuate the perspective of this huge interior space in a way that recalls the market hall of Ferentino.

On this rectangular esplanade (approximately 130 by 98 meters), two stories of columned porticoes (the upper story set slightly back) frame the *temenos* on three sides, leaving the larger side open toward the valley. This vast, oblong U-shaped colonnade acts as a setting for the temple proper on its high podium. A broad stairway led up to the octostyle facade in one sweep. The *cavea* of the theater was situated centrally in front of the temple at the bottom of this stairway, as at Palestrina.

A theater crowns the monument
At the summit of the temple of Praeneste, the *cavea* facing the valley survives where the Palazzo Barberini stands today. This was built in 1640, in place of and on the site of the semicircular ambulatory that crowned the whole complex.

Temple and Theater

The two sanctuaries which Sulla built present a similar organic link between theater and temple. An understanding of the meaning of this close association between a *cavea* and a holy of holies is essential to an understanding of the function of the two buildings. In fact, the juxtaposition is confusing, so much so that a historian of Roman architecture of the stature of William L. MacDonald could refer, when writing of Praeneste, to a "large theater-like hemicycle."

To understand the meaning of Sulla's architectural scheme, it is necessary to remember the importance that the religion of the Hellenistic rulers held for the dictator, in view of his monarchical aspirations. This was clearly his source of inspiration. Remember as well that the sanctuary at Tivoli was dedicated to Hercules Victor, a god with whom victorious Sulla identified himself, as Greek monarchs had done since Alexander following in the footsteps of his father, Philip II.

On this subject, a passage from Ernst Kantorowicz in *The Two Bodies of the King*, in turn taken from Diodorus, is illuminating. "While King Philip II of Macedonia was sitting down in his seat in the theater of Aigai (or Edessa, capital of the kingdom) statues of the twelve gods were brought into the theater in procession, with one of Philip figuring as the thirteenth god." It would appear that from the fourth century B.C. onward, the theater had an influence on the liturgy for the deification of the sovereign. In order to facilitate the court ritual, the theater formed an organic whole with the temple, a time-honored custom that was established during the Hellenistic reigns, probably inspired by Near-Eastern rulers.

A similar phenomenon occurred in 55 B.C. when Pompey built the first permanent theater in Rome itself, in conjunction with the temple of Venus Victrix. This sanctuary dominated the theater to such an overwhelming extent that "the steps of the *cavea* looked like a grandiose staircase leading up to the temple" (Karl Schefold). Pompey's theater, little of which survives today, introduced the formula of a *cavea* built by way of superposed arcades and semicircular concentric vaulting rather than hewn out of a hillside. This solution, typically Roman in both materials and techniques, was to apply equally to theaters and amphitheaters. Pompey's huge creation embodied an extraordinary technological revolution representing the first large-scale construction of semicircular supports radiating outward. In addition, the vaults followed the concave shape of the *cavea*'s tiers. From this time, all the basic elements of Roman architecture were present, giving rise to one of the most innovative schools of building. Its creations were not to fall short of its early promise. Besides the temple-theater, the building which Pompey erected in the Campus Martius behind the stage wall consisted of a vast quadriporticus with a double row of columns. In this way, the grandiose rectangular complex, closed on the short western side by the hemicycle of the theater, measured some 320 by 160 meters. Its lofty structure, almost 40 meters high, towered over the surrounding buildings.

In dedicating the temple overlooking the *cavea* to Venus Victrix, Pompey aligned himself with a succession of figures who had placed themselves under the protection of this quintessentially Roman goddess. Sulla had invoked the aid of Venus Felix, and Caesar had worshipped Venus Genitrix in the temple of his forum. A similar intention to that of Sulla with the sanctuary of Fortuna at Praeneste or with the temple of Hercules Victor at Tivoli is evident here. In representing himself as Venus's chosen one, Pompey was asserting himself as a candidate for heroic status. With his secret aspirations to the title of emperor, if not king, the Princeps Senatus was paving the way to his deification through his attainment of absolute power.

It should be noted that the general arrangement of this complex built by Pompey in Rome, with the quadriporticus adjoining the *cavea* and the sanctuary standing at the latter's highest point, begs deliberate comparison with the

Temple of Jupiter at Terracina
The axonometric view of the sanctuary of Jupiter Anxur at Terracina, built on an artificial terrace overlooking the sea, shows the free placement of the temple and the portico which has disappeared, on top of the vaulted substructures of the complex.

Roman plan of the theater of Pompey
The plan of the theater of Pompey, shown on a fragment of marble of the *Forma urbis* (or plan of ancient Rome executed during the reign of Septimius Severus between 203 and 211). At the top of the *cavea* stood the temple of Venus Victrix, dominating the sacred complex.

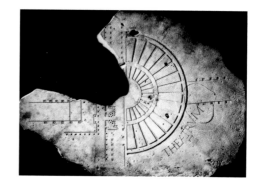

Page 33
Vaulted substructures
The arcades of the vaulted substructures of the sanctuary at Terracina. The esplanade is supported by concrete vaults with a reticulated covering and quoins at the angles.

Page 34

Succession of arches beneath the temple of Jupiter
Perspectival view of the supporting arches that surround the terrace of the temple of Jupiter Anxur at Terracina, dating from around 80 B.C. These arches, perpendicular to the large arcade visible from the outside, guarantee a perfect buttressing of the structure.

Cryptoporticus of the temple
Behind the large external arcade, the supporting structure built at Terracina consists of a vast hall for civic use (cryptoporticus), with a barrel vault built out of concrete. This is supported by walls with a reticulated surface. Toward the outside, semicircular bays – alternately in the form of windows and doors – provide lighting and permit the free movement of people in this huge underground hall.

representation of the universe as seen by the ancients. The inhabited world, the *oikoumene*, is square; above this, spheres, one inside the other, were arranged around the earth, for it was this that the semicircular tiers of the *cavea* symbolized; finally, the temple, with its apse symbolizing the assembly of the gods dominating the cosmos, completes the whole. The sanctuary evoked the divinities that regulated humanity, with Virtus, Honor, and Felicitas mentioned by name. It was in effect an *imago mundi*. Such a site fully justifies Pompey's reputation as an initiator of grand building projects. He merits Pliny's assertion that as the "one and only Princeps and victor of Mithridates, he not only equalled the exploits of Alexander the Great, but almost attained those of Hercules and Dionysos." It is clear here that a great step had been made toward the deification of the living ruler.

By the end of the Republic, the techniques of construction had made huge advances through the generalized use of *opus caementicum* in place of cut stone. A semiological language had also asserted itself with, in Pierre Gros's words, "an increased number of buildings of an essentially symbolic and dynastico-religious character, together with an independent development of a monumentality that seems to feed off itself."

An Eloquent System

If the *cavea* associated with the sanctuary, at Praeneste as at Tivoli, played such a clear role in the process of deification of the Princeps, one can appreciate the anxiety aroused in the capital itself by the creation of victorious Pompey's temple-theater. By condemning this first permanent theater in the capital, his critics attacked the meaning it embodied rather than the notion that the population would in some way be perverted by grand spectacle. The very evocation of royalty revulsed the Senate. Such a fear indeed was to lead to the murder of Julius Caesar in 44 B.C.

The temple-theater conjunction was not isolated or coincidental in the case of Praeneste, Tivoli and Pompey's theater in Rome. In fact, the same formula can be found on the site of the temple of Juno at Gabii, near Praeneste, that dates back to 200 B.C. Surrounded by a columned portico on three sides of a rectangular esplanade, this sanctuary with its hexastyle facade stood centrally in front of a *cavea*. Indeed, the formula already seemed customary, as Luigi Crema indicates, in the case of the Punic temple of Cagliari in Sardinia. Dating from the third century B.C., this sanctuary could have been inspired by certain Hellenistic religious theaters. So could the temple of Pietrabbondante, a Samnite town to the east of Rome, where the building was constructed of white marble, another feature illustrating Greek influence.

The organic link between temple and theater of a ritual nature, based on the worship of royalty, forms a constant factor that is of great significance. It characterizes the period when court ritual penetrated Roman territory, inspired by the practice of the deification of sovereigns, adopted by Diadochian courts.

This configuration continued up to the second century A.D., at the Spanish site of Manigua, near Seville, where a vast complex, similar to that of Praeneste, sat on the flank of a hill, with terraces, stairways, long converging ramps, and an upper esplanade, reached by means of a semicircular *cavea* leading to an oblong sanctuary at the summit. This complex may have had some connection with the cult of the emperor Hadrian, a native of this region of Baetica.

These examples show that architectural forms can teach us about the preoccupations, intentions, and ambitions of people. In a vocabulary that overcame censorship more easily, in a way that texts could not do, these creations unlock an unspoken truth that authors could not reveal, given the taboo in Rome regarding certain matters dealing with the subject of power.

Axonometric reconstruction of the temple of Hercules Victor at Tivoli
The main terrace, on the edge of a ravine, is 130 by 98 meters and consists of a terrace surrounded on three sides by double, two-story porticoes, on a substructure similar to that of Terracina. In the center stood an octostyle temple behind the *cavea* of a central theater. The complex dates from Sulla's time, around 80 B.C.

Mosaic of the flooding of the Nile
In the room forming the nymphaeum at Palestrina was a huge, sumptuous mosaic representing the flooding of the Nile. The allusion to Egypt is linked to the cult of Isis, whose popularity in the Roman world was rising sharply at that time. This detail shows a temple with curved roof (Egyptian) behind a gathering of soldiers and a priestess beneath the shade of a *velum*. The mosaic dates from the first century B.C. (Museo Prenestino Barberiniano, Palestrina)

EARLY IMPERIAL ART

Augustan Architecture
and the Process of Romanization

Page 39
Portrait of Octavian-Augustus
This marble, dating from the
beginning of the modern era,
shows the Princeps crowned with
a garland of myrtle leaves, characterized by his fine, determined
features. (Capitoline Museum,
Rome)

After the masterpieces marking the end of the Republican era under Sulla, a
period of political instability during Pompey's and Caesar's rule caused an acceler-
ation in both the stylistic development of Roman architecture and in the urbaniza-
tion of the capital.

The construction of Caesar's forum revolutionized the layout of official Rome.
By placing the series of major buildings north of the Clivus Argentarius that were
to culminate in the works of Apollodorus in the second century A.D., the Forum
Iulium (or Forum of Caesar) determined the evolution of the city until the late
Empire, by virtue of its vast dimensions (160 by 75 meters). The forum consisted
of a rectangular area placed on a southeast-northwest axis, composed of long porticoes with double rows of columns running along either side. At one end of the
square stood the octostyle temple of Venus Genitrix.

In fact this ambitious program functioned on both an architectural and semiological level. The forum is primarily an *agora*, a public place, surrounded by porticoes functioning as *stoai*. At the end of the square, the construction of the temple
dedicated to Venus Genitrix bestowed the qualities of a *temenos* on this urban
place, transforming the public space into a religious space. It was created with a
dynastic purpose, there being no issue as a result of the violent death of its
founder. Nevertheless, it asserted itself more as a manifestation of monarchical
power than as a municipal building. This is why its design was emulated by Augustus and Vespasian, and then by Nerva and Trajan. The forum's vigorous impact on
the layout of the city was to be like a pole to later enterprises that involved the
organization of Rome's center.

The Forum of Augustus

The arrival of the imperial era marked a decisive change in every way. The leaders
of the Julio-Claudian and Flavian dynasties would give a considerable boost to
architecture, with a dramatic evolution in Rome itself, where each emperor sought
to leave a visible mark of his reign. Thus, Octavian (Augustus) founded his own
forum adjoining, and perpendicular to, Julius Caesar's forum. Caesar's tragic
death was still too recent for the project not to reflect the event. Although it was
started in 31 B.C., the sanctuary forming the center of the forum was not consecrated until 2 B.C. Dedicated to Mars, the god of war, it bore the name *ultor*
("avenger"), in reference to Caesar's death.

The Forum of Augustus covers over a hectare (125 by 85 meters). At the end of
the square, lined on both sides by two columned porticoes, the temple stood on a
high platform, with an octostyle facade similar to the temple in the Forum Iulium.
The interior of its wide *cella* was punctuated on either side by seven semi-
detached columns. These formed six side niches, a formula that introduced the
solution Rabirius would adopt for the throne room known as the *aula regia*, in
Domitian's Domus Flavia. A major feature of this forum resides in the two vast
semicircular exedras on either side of the temple of Mars Ultor. These two

**Stucco found beneath
the Farnesina**
Stucco decoration from a ceiling
of the Roman villa found beneath
the Farnesina. This winged
Victory, dating from 19 B.C.,
from an Attic workshop is part
of a cycle dedicated to initiation
to the mysteries of Dionysos.
The elegance of Augustan art is
apparent here. (Museo nazionale,
Rome)

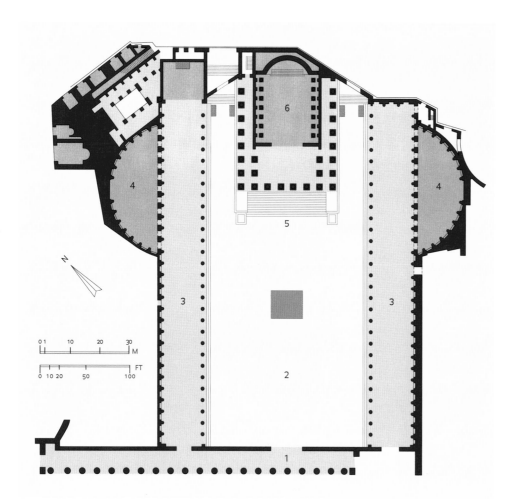

exedras, of basilical type, are symmetrical. Facing each other across the facade of the temple, they formed curves in the walls surrounding the whole complex. Apollodorus later adopted this formula, detail for detail, in the Forum of Trajan. Their importance suggests that they embodied a meaning beyond their simple aesthetic effect or their role of secular basilicas.

Remember that there were also two *exedras* at Praeneste, structures exclusive to Roman architecture. When adjoined to a temple, their purpose was greater than that of a location for meetings, learning, or judicial confrontation.

The importance given to these curvilinear structures in the Forum of Augustus prompts a religious interpretation of their sumptuous construction in marble, with their two superposed stories of porticoes arranged in a semicircle where statues of great men were placed as a sort of sacred monument. They were honorific structures, halls with a commemorative function. Here we must surmise their meaning because philologists are not much help. They will not hazard any conjecture that is not backed up by texts, and ancient authors were not in the habit of qualifying architectural spaces.

We know that the porticoes, the first story of which was decorated with a row of caryatids (copied from those of the Erechtheion in Athens), housed a collection of works of art, some of them created for Alexander the Great. It included sculptures, paintings, and even a bronze chariot. The references to Attic art and to works from the Acropolis bear testimony to Augustus's orthodox taste. The connection with Alexander made an allusion to the autocratic ambitions of the Princeps who had, like his predecessor, created a building of a dynastic nature. If the reference to Caesar, adoptive father of Octavian (Augustus), is explicit, the allusion to the condemnation of his assassins is not enough to hide the monarchical symbolism of this religious monument.

Painting of the Augustan period
Detail of a wallpainting from the villa discovered beneath the Farnesina in Rome, depicting Dionysian mysteries: the infant Dionysos in the lap of a nymph. This work, dating from 19 B.C., illustrates the refinement of painting during the imperial Augustan period. (Museo Nazionale Romano, Rome)

The home of Augustus on the Palatine
The Hall of Masks in the house of Augustus on the Palatine. Excavated in 1969 and the results recently published, this dwelling, dating from 25 B.C. is decorated with paintings in the second Pompeian style. They depict theatrical scenes, or *scaenae frontes*, with a single vanishing point and a strictly symmetrical perspective.

In the *exedras*, the statues of great ancestors almost served as a political state-
ment. To the left was a group showing Aeneas carrying his father, Anchises, and
holding his son, Ascanius, by the hand. To the right, the figure of Romulus, son of
Mars, recalled the foundation of Rome. In the *cella* of the temple, it appears that a
statue of Caesar deified was placed next to statues of Mars and Venus. Finally, at
the end of the left portico, the Sala del Colosseo was decorated, perhaps during
the Claudian era, with a huge statue of Augustus himself.

Indeed, Augustus's program in the forum had an emblematic meaning, as the
temple dedicated to Mars Ultor suggests. In addition to the statues of famous
figures, the temple contained the standards of the defeated Parthian legions.
Thus, the temple symbolically avenged both the death of Caesar and the defeat at
Carrhae in 53. This didactic forum was thus a monument to memory. Its creator did
not limit himself to glorifying the past. He also celebrated the birth of the principate.

The Austerity of Augustus

By dedicating this forum to Caesar's spirits, Augustus showed that he had no fear
of being the object of criticism. He was doing justice to his spiritual father without
laying himself open to the disapproval of the senators, who were always ready to
condemn aspirations to royalty and the religious worship of rulers. As a result, he
allowed himself a free rein in the marble and cipolin adornment of its colonnades
and peristyles.

On a personal level, the head of the empire demonstrated great simplicity and
moral rigor. Although he lived on the Palatine hill, his home was relatively simple.
And although it contained rooms with wall paintings in the second Pompeian
style, its dimensions were modest, almost small, in size. It was not the palace of a
Pontifex Maximus or of an all-powerful *Imperator*.

Water reserves of the fleet
At the tip of the cape of Misenum, to the west of Pozzuoli and the bay of Naples, the Roman fleet's base was a port formed by semi-submerged craters. The Piscina Mirabile, dating from the Augustan period, is a huge covered cistern, 70 by 25.5 meters, consisting of 48 cruciform pillars. This huge area enabled the fleet to stock reserves of fresh water.

This same sort of reticence was evident in his attitude to the distinctions that people wished to bestow upon him. When he became emperor, Augustus dedicated his home to Vesta, but he refused to be the object of a cult, although the Senate had added a pediment to his house, symbol of a temple, and had had planted on either side of the entrance a laurel, the tree of Apollo.

An anecdote illustrates Augustus's fear of opponents of monarchy. When Agrippa built a temple in the emperor's honor in 27 B.C. and sought to place a statue of him there, a clear manifestation of deification, Augustus had flatly refused. The temple was therefore dedicated to the gods in general and became the first Pantheon, to be replaced in Hadrian's time, a century and a half later, by the building that we admire today under the same name.

Clearly Augustus steadfastly and consistently rejected the symbols of absolute power.

Romanization

From the third century B.C., Rome tended to unite under its leadership the neighboring populations in order to form a unified power. First it was the Italic tribes, then the Greek colonies of southern Italy and Sicily who constituted the Roman

Page 46

A cistern still in operation
The underground cistern of Albano, still in use, is a good example of the urban infrastructure of the Romans. Built at the end of the second century, this construction, known by the name of Cisternone, supplied the army in the Castra Albana.

The nymphaeum of Cicero's villa
In the ancient Roman city of Formia, on the bay of Gaeta, a patrician villa, thought to be that of Cicero, possesses a fine nymphaeum. It probably dates from the beginning of the Empire. The underground building consists of a barrel vault in concrete, with coffering and ribs. This ceiling is supported on columns separating the main chamber from the lateral buildings on either side.

world. At an early stage, Roman legions clashed with the Punic expansionism of the Carthaginians. Only by pouring all its resources into winning did Rome finally achieve victory. During these conflicts, strategic necessity led to the occupation of Provence, in Gaul, and then of Spain.

To the east, Greece soon fell before the onslaughts of the Roman generals, and their forces went on to penetrate Asia Minor (province of Asia in 170 B.C.) and the Near East, colonizing vast provinces there. But then Rome came into contact with the Parthians, always a formidable opponent.

This extraordinary progress toward the unification of the Mediterranean region (*mare nostrum*) eventually led to the conquest Egypt and the Mesopotamian provinces under Trajan, as well as the invasion of the Germanic and Danubian regions, and even Britain. This colossal appetite for domination became greedier as Roman strength became increasingly invincible. By the time of the arrival of Augustus, Rome had developed a policy of rampant imperialism, no longer recognizing any limit to its ambitions.

Rome imposed itself not only by force but also by a system of civilization whose most visible sign was the town, with its particular layout and specific architecture. This urban development was only one of many lasting aspects of the process of land planning. It extended to the entire landscape, encompassing ground leveling, road and bridge construction, and, in particular, aqueducts, which were indispensable for sustaining urban life, industry, and land irrigation. This human dominance over nature featured huge projects of marshland drainage, reclamation of swamps, and the use of rivers for shipping and developing safe ports, equipped with jetties, warehouses, and cisterns, for both merchant and naval fleets.

Rome thus subjected both the Italic peninsula proper and the provinces, near and far, to its spirit of strict organization, making a homogeneous, coherent whole out of them. It imposed its mark on the entire Western world. Aerial photography today reveals the traces of the great Roman roads and the system of centuriation, dividing up the landscape as if enmeshed in a vast net thrown over the conquered regions.

The creation of rapid communication routes resulted in rectilinear roads over huge distances. We can still admire the way they cross coastal plains, especially considering how basic the technical means were at the disposal of the land surveyors at that time, who used geographic maps to plan the most direct connections. Despite the unevenness of the terrain, the main roads followed their course, across countryside and marshes, over rivers and tributaries to the sea. They overcame the irregularities in their path with embankments and bridges, excavating hills and slopes and always applying the most efficient solutions.

Town Planning and Centuriation

The system that governed Roman town planning was based on two perpendicular axes forming a right angle, the *cardo* (north-south) and the *decumanus* (east-west), intersecting at the forum. In its perpendicular organization, this scheme is derived from both Hippodamian town planning and the Etruscan city (Hippodamos of Miletus rebuilt his own town in the fifth century B.C. and then established the plan of Piraeus. He is acknowledged as the inventor of the rectilinear town plan.) These two factors probably jointly influenced the disposition later adopted by Roman legions' camps. Actually, the orthogonal plan goes back much earlier to the Middle Kingdom in Egypt (around 2000 B.C.). Indeed, the necropolises of the Old Kingdom surrounding the great pyramids (around 2600 B.C.) already indicated that cities of the living could have been organized on a grid pattern.

Such a design of squared units did not apply to Rome, an ancient Italic city, where the primitive town had been shaped by huts arranged with no particular scheme. But it was employed for new cities, built from scratch (as in the case of Timgad), based on programs undertaken with military or economic considerations in mind.

This system soon extended beyond urban limits. For colonial purposes (the distribution of land to war veterans), it underwent a rigorous process of centuriation. Alongside the road network, established from the fourth century B.C. onward, the land was divided up into square units measuring 2400 feet a side (700 meters). This system spread over the entire Roman world. Squaring was applied the length of the via Appia (Appius was censor in 312 B.C.) all the way to Capua, and then extended in 270–225 to Taranto and Brindisi. Squaring is also visible on the route of the via Flaminia that led to Narni, an extension built in 299 reaching Spoleto. The via Aurelia, which led to Modena and Aquilea and was built in 177, also bears the signs of it, as do many other roads, in North Africa and in Spain. Road construction everywhere was accompanied by the process of romanization and planning.

Subsequently, the dense grid of these roads, military and commercial alike, spread throughout the Empire at the same time that centuriation reached the fertile plains of the Mediterranean basin, today visible in aerial surveys. These rationalizing systems imposed their mark on the land; Rome "humanized" the environment and asserted its primacy in order to promote development. A town that

Plan of a Roman camp
This layout of a typical Roman camp *(castrum)* shows the organization adopted by the troops during their campaigns in hostile territory. Two legions would build the camp around the *praetorium* of the general occupying the center. The camp was composed of a rectangular enclosure, with four centrally placed gates, which corresponded to the *cardo* and *decumanus*. "It is in the organization of the camp that one should seek the origins of Roman military architecture during the Empire" (Pierre Grimal).

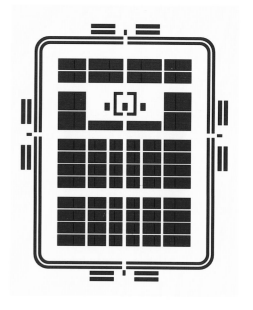

The aqueduct of Nîmes crossing the River Gardon
In itself a symbol of the remarkable capabilities of Roman engineers, the famous Pont du Gard is in fact an aqueduct 300 meters long. Its three levels of arcades total around 50 meters in height over the Gardon. The structure supplying water to the city of Nîmes was built during Agrippa's reign, in 19 B.C. It is a model of technology, combining the science of the engineer with the artistry of the architect.

developed anarchically was a malediction in the eyes of the Republican censors. Henceforward, careful organization would be seen as a universal panacea, capable of extending well-being and prosperity to all citizens.

This is why the urban plan, with its main components of forum, capitol (in Rome's image), temples dedicated to the protector gods, utilitarian buildings — markets, ports, warehousing — (*emporium*), cryptoporticuses, workshops, fountains, and recreational centers — baths, nymphaea, theater, amphitheater, circus, gardens and pools —, was the major preoccupation of the *aediles*, a role often assumed by the rulers themselves. Rome disseminated the model of its urban organization, and each town in the Empire aspired to recreate, on its own scale, the facilities of the metropolis for the prosperity of its citizens.

Road infrastructure of Provence
Typical of the Roman road system, the Julian Bridge (le Pont Julien), built in large blocks of stone without mortar, has a remarkably elegant overall design, with its large, central arch echoed by symmetrical lateral arches. Two open bays which lighten the structure are set in the piers. The roadway is only slightly cambered. The bridge was built around A.D. 10 on the Roman road that passed through Apt (Apta Julia).

Landmark of Roman roadbuilding
More emblematic in its design,
the Flavian Bridge in Provence has
only one arch, but the road it
bears is marked by two triumphal
arches with Corinthian pilasters.
It was built around A.D. 70, during
Vespasian's reign.

The Development of Provence

In the Empire, Provence, the southern part of Gaul, enjoyed an early development
because of its strategic position in relation to Spain. Under Augustus — actually,
under the governership of Agrippa (63–12 B.C.), Augustus's right-hand man to
whom Gaul was entrusted from 20 to 19 B.C. in order to build the road system and
the public infrastructure — the south of France enjoyed a considerable boom.
Many constructions – bridges, aqueducts, cryptoporticuses – were created during
the century that started with the appointment of Agrippa up to the beginning of
the Flavian dynasty.

Probably the most spectacular Roman creation in Provence is the aqueduct
known as the Pont du Gard, whose three levels of monumental arcades cross the
river Gardon to guarantee the supply of water to the town of Nîmes. Built in 19
B.C., the aqueduct spans the valley, almost 300 meters long and 50 meters high
above the river. It is entirely built of large stone blocks with no mortar. This is but
the most spectacular element in a 50-kilometer water channel, engineered with
only the slightest gradient, between 0.25 and 0.5 percent, that still amazes modern technicians. In the domain where architecture connects power and religion,
the Maison Carrée at Nîmes, built between 15 and 12 B.C. during Augustus's
reign, is numbered among the best preserved of Roman temples in the entire
Empire. The building stands on a high podium with a flight of steps at the front.
Dedicated to the worship of the imperial family (Augustus, Livia, and the two sons
of Agrippa, Caius and Lucius), it is a pseudo-peripteral hexastyle temple measuring 14 by 28 meters. The columns at the corners of the facade are 50 feet apart
and those at the corner of the side are 100 feet apart. Its clear, precise decoration,

The Maison Carrée at Nîmes
A detail of the very classical ornamentation of the Maison Carrée, with its delicately sculpted Corinthian columns, its entablature, and its frieze of ornamental foliage under the row of dentils.

Temple of imperial worship
The Maison Carrée is a Vitruvian hexastyle temple that formed the center of the Forum of Nîmes. Its remarkable state of preservation is due to its early subsequent use as a church. The sanctuary, built during Augustus's reign between 15 and 12 B.C. was dedicated to the emperor, to his wife Livia, and to the two sons of Agrippa, Caius and Lucius. This dynastic temple is characterized by elegance, despite the presence of embedded columns around the *cella*. Today, the Carrée d'Art, designed by the architect Norman Foster, stands next to it.

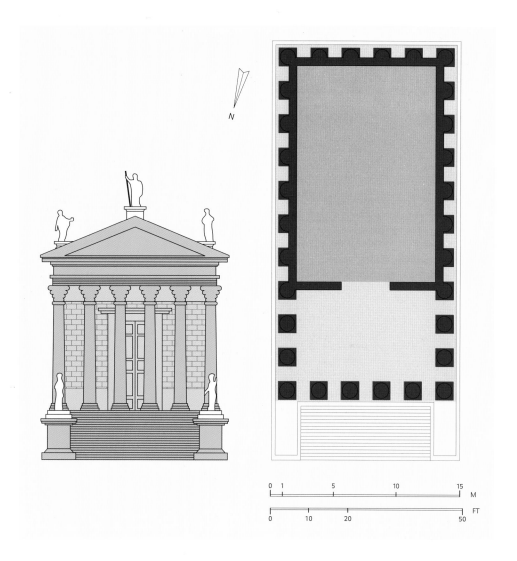

The Maison Carrée
Elevation and plan of the Maison Carrée at Nîmes. The hexastyle structure on a high podium presents ten freestanding columns forming the vestibule and twenty engaged columns around the *cella*. The area of this peristyle equals two squares: the length of its colonnade is double its width (100 by 50 Roman feet of 0.29 meters each).

with its Tuscan Corinthian capitals, constitutes a perfect exemple of the Vitruvian approach in its most classical form. Forming the center of a huge square, the temple was surrounded by porticoes delimiting the edge of a forum, which no longer exists.

At Vienne, another Vitruvian hexastyle temple was built in A.D. 15 and dedicated to Augustus and Rome, joined together in common veneration. The style of the building is as sharp and austere as the temple at Nîmes. The idea of associating the state (or the city that embodied it completely) with the representative of power would be repeated many times in the future. Augustus, whilst careful to show restraint in the outward manifestations of autocracy displayed in Rome, did not observe the same timidity in the provinces. The garden of the Fountain of Nemausus in Nîmes is a nymphaeum dedicated to the glory of Augustus. Restored between 1739 and 1753 during Louis XIV's reign, this sacred fountain consists of a triple pool. First is the spring itself, where two Roman *exedras* survive, with the water held back by a dam. Then there is a central pool with, in its center, a large altar in the shape of a rectangular island, surrounded by supporting porticoes in the role of nymphaeum. At each corner of the altar stood a column symbolizing the limits of the world, with perhaps a colossal statue of the prince originally standing in the middle. Finally, another pool received the water, which was then canalized toward the center of the town. Similarly to the Maison Carrée, a triple colonnade built in Hadrian's time surrounded the complex on three sides, with the fourth side, to the north, formed by the hill at the foot of which the spring welled up, and which flanks the theater. On the west side of the complex, the so-called temple of Diana, built in A.D. 75, in Vespasian's time, possesses an interesting barrel vault with transverse ribs in stone blocks. The *cella* (central chamber), with

Page 55
The town of Vienne reveres Augustus
Hexastyle facade of the temple of Vienne, dedicated to Augustus and Rome. It was finished in A.D. 15, one year after the death of the sovereign. As at Nîmes, the elegance of the building's Roman Corinthian style derives from rules decreed by Vitruvius.

The Theoretical Misapprehensions of Vitruvius

By virtue of its size, the Forum of Augustus (inaugurated in 2 B.C.) earned its place in the succession of innovations initiated by the sanctuaries at Palestrina and Tivoli with their vaults and curvilinear designs. This art remained for the most part overlooked by Vitruvius, the only Roman theorist on architecture whose works have survived.

Author of a ten-volume treatise in Latin on the art of building, entitled *De Architectura*, Vitruvius has fascinated generations of historians who have attempted to discern within his work the laws of Roman aesthetics concerning temples, theaters, basilicas, and funerary monuments.

Blessed with exceptional fame since a manuscript of his work was rediscovered in 1415 by Poggio Bracciolini in the abbey library of Saint Gall, Vitruvius was to be the object of a first Latin edition published in 1486. The greatest architects of the Renaissance fed on this manna. It was commented on, illustrated and codified. Notably, in 1537, Serlio defined the classical orders of architecture by basing himself on Vitruvius.

My assertion in the introduction to this book that Roman architecture is one of the most important in history might seem to be provocative, given what Vitruvius writes. Despite the magnitude of the creations, the number of monuments, their quality in both spatial and technical terms, it has been fashionable, until fairly recent times, to denigrate Roman art, seeing in it nothing but a by-product of Greek art — indeed, an overblown, bastardized version of Hellenic buildings that were universally admired and revered. These critics did not always perceive the originality and innovative nature of Roman architecture.

Forty years ago, some critics still viewed Rome's creations as awkward and tasteless copies of the classical aesthetic — a plagiarism of the creations of Athens, Olympia, or Delphi, all ultimate yardsticks of quality. Art history has had to overcome this myopia, based partly on interpretations of Vitruvius's writings. *De Architectura* indeed prompted some serious errors of judgment.

Vitruvian thought, reflecting that of its Greek precursors, did not recognize the novelty of the grandiose enterprises at the end of the Republican era. Indeed, major constructions built less than 50 years before Vitruvius published his book, are not even mentioned. The author must have been aware of the fantastic creations of the temple of Fortuna at Praeneste and the temple of Hercules Victor at Tivoli, both barely a day's ride from Rome. Why did he not discuss them? Was the name of Sulla taboo, his reign an object of general disapproval because of his monarchist leanings? Or did these vast compositions simply not correspond to the aesthetic theories of the author, imbued with Hellenic, rather than Hellenistic, conceptions?

Whatever the reason, this Vitruvian omission is at the root of a serious misapprehension. For a long time, it prevented architectural historians from understanding the essentials of Roman style. This was further compounded by a chronological error: during the Renaissance, scholars, for the most part philologians, dated Vitruvius to a much later period in the second or even third century A.D., whereas we now know that he was born in 88 B.C. and died in 26 B.C., during a period of fundamental change. When he published his *Ten Books on Architecture* around 31 B.C., Vitruvius could not have known the majority of Augustus's creations, or those of Tiberius or Nero, or the art of the Flavians, in particular of Domitian, not to mention the works of Trajan and Hadrian during the Antonine dynasty, which are the apogee of Roman architectural creativity. It was therefore impossible for his treatise to reflect the essential contribution of Rome.

The misunderstanding caused by Vitruvius's work continued to grow until the beginning of the twentieth century. His commentators are responsible for the notion that Rome was but a continuation, "on a grand scale", of Greek art. They give authority to the illusion that the architectural orders, Doric, Ionic, Corinthian, and Tuscan, are essential characteristics of Roman art, a concept on which academic teaching was founded. But if Rome took inspiration from the Greek orders, without giving them a truly structural role, their role must have been mainly orna-

mental. The essence of architectural thought was elsewhere: in the creation of space achieved by the arch, the vault, and, above all, the dome. Vitruvius does not explore this aspect.

De Architectura had other repercussions as well. Appearing at the dawn of Empire, this text was perhaps at the root of a certain restraint in Roman architecture. In dedicating his work to Augustus, Vitruvius encouraged the timidity of the early stages of Augustan art. In keeping with the attitude of caution that he was always to maintain toward manifestations of outward power, Augustus shunned any ostentation in the capital, since he knew that the senators were against it. Consequently, he took a reserved, cautious approach to anything that might betray his autocratic ambitions. A theorist like Vitruvius, professing a sincere distrust of anything new, could not fail to confirm such an attitude. In fact, Vitruvius advocated a classicizing, traditionalist style in a neo-Attic mode that temporarily froze the dynamic creativity of the Roman designers of the end of the Republican era. Grandiose architecture regained its momentum only gradually with the Forum of Augustus and gave itself a free rein only from the reign of Nero onward.

The writings of Vitruvius remain important nevertheless. One only has to look at the resurgence of studies dedicated to him, as stressed by Pierre Gros in an international conference organized by the Ecole française in Rome. *De Architectura* is to be republished in three new editions: a German one that "will completely reassess the accepted ideas"; a French one that will establish a more reliable original text, with "many revisions, some of them overwhelming"; and an Italian one that will give "a new vigor to Vitruvian thought." Concurrently, studies are investigating his knowledge of machines, discovering "a technical Vitruvius, descendant of the Hellenistic engineers".

The fact nevertheless remains that we cannot hope to find in Vitruvius whatever he overlooked: the essence of the Roman spirit of architecture, that is, the capacity to conceive and to achieve creations that were spatially original, by means of the arch, the vault and the dome.

Right top and bottom

Sanctuary of the sacred spring

To the west of the Nymphaeum of Nemausus stands the Temple of Diana, which was part of the additions made later, during the Flavian dynasty or during Hadrian's time. This splendid vaulted construction, whose barrel vault is reinforced by transverse ribs, consists of side niches between which embedded columns form projections. These blind bays are decorated with alternately curved and triangular pediments.

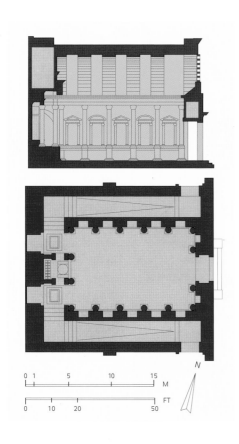

0 1   5   10   15
                          M

0   10   20   50
                          FT

N

Longitudinal section and plan of the so-called Temple of Diana at Nîmes

The *cella*, with its three "chapels of worship," is flanked on both sides by vaulted ramps providing access to the roof and also performing a buttressing role.

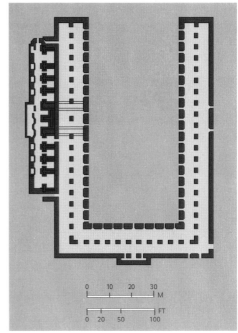

Top left

The underground halls of Arles
The cryptoporticuses of Arles, with their galleries of flattened arches, form a vast underground complex situated beneath the Forum of the Roman town. Consisting of three galleries with double bays, the cryptoporticuses, discovered around 40 years ago, represent a grandiose creation, whose precise function remains uncertain.

Top right

Beneath the Forum of Arles: a hidden world
The plan of the cryptoporticuses of Arles shows a U-shaped arrangement, with two galleries almost 90 meters long, joined perpendicularly by a third gallery 60 meters long.

The triumphal arch at Orange
Built in A.D. 20, the triumphal arch at Orange (Arausio) commemorates a victory over a chieftain of Gaul. Situated on the *cardo* of the town, it consists of three bays, with the central one flanked by narrower lateral entrances. Sculptures representing battles between Romans and Gauls decorate all sides of the arch.

The amphitheater of Nîmes
Known as "les Arènes", the amphitheater built during the Flavian dynasty, forms an oval 133 by 101 meters. Its facade, at a height of 21 meters, is made up of two levels, each comprising 60 arcades. It could accommodate 24 000 spectators on its 34 rows of seating. The outwardly visible structure is entirely built in large blocks of stone, assembled without mortar. The lower arcades are separated by pilasters. On the upper level, embedded Doric columns enliven the ornamentation.

In the wings of the arena
Access to the seating is made through vaulted corridors underpinning the building leading to the *vomitoria* (entrances). The construction of elliptical vaults and arches posed problems of stereotomy that demonstrate the virtuosity of the Roman stonemasons.

The theater at Orange
The theater of Orange, among the best preserved of the Empire, was built during the reigns of Tiberus and Claudius. The importance of this building resides in the stage building 37 meters high that survives intact, apart from the ornamentation of the *frons scaenae* whose three stories of columns have disappeared. The *cavea* is set into the hill, which was hollowed out for this , according to the Greek custom. In this, the theater differs from the formulas perfected in Rome with the theater of Pompey, entirely supported by superposed arcades.

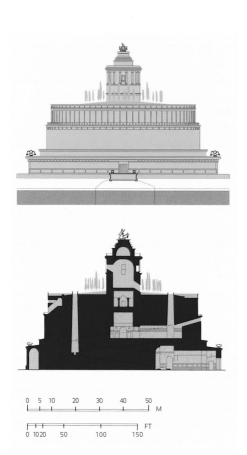

Mausoleums and Funerary Monuments

The Romans showed great imagination in the field of funerary architecture. There exist tombs in the form of round towers, tumuli, chapels, tall spires, underground burial chambers; the list is endless. The most impressive is the mausoleum, which, while remaining faithful to Etruscan tradition, assumed huge proportions. A number of circular constructions, inspired by the original tumulus of Cerveteri, fit into this category.

This type already existed in the Republican period. In North Africa, the tomb known as the Tombeau de la Chrétienne near Tipasa is a huge construction dating from the first century B.C. On a cylindrical base, punctuated by embedded columns, the mass of this distinguished monument stands tall, crowned by a cone built of large blocks of stone.

Similarly circular in form, the mausoleum of Augustus in Rome, begun in A.D. 14 and not finished until A.D. 28, was a substantial work, 87 meters in diameter. It consisted of five concentric structures increasingly elevated as they approached the center: the top of the tumulus, covered in vegetation, reached 44.5 meters. A vaulted passage gave access to the chamber of the *gens Julia*.

During the Antonine period, the principle of the circular tumulus-tomb was revived for Hadrian's mausoleum. Its construction began in 130. Decorated with pilasters, the cylindrical monument, 64 meters in diameter, stood on a square podium-base measuring more than 80 meters across. Above, on the tree-covered tumulus, stood a cubic structure crowned by Apollo's quadriga. Inside the solid structure, a vaulted hallway led to a heliocoidal passage to the central funerary chamber. A bridge over the Tiber stands before this huge surviving edifice, later transformed into a fortress under the name of Castel San Angelo.

Another category of tomb, bearing some resemblance to Hadrian's mausoleum, consisted of a towerlike structure, as in the famous mausoleum of Cecilia Metella, dating from 30 B.C., built on the side of the Appian Way, or as in the contemporary tomb of the Plautii not far from Tivoli. The largest of these monuments is that of Munatius Plancus (Praetor of Caesar in 43 B.C.), which crowns the head-

From classical tomb to fortress
On the Via Appia, the tomb of
Cecilia Metella, dating from 30
B.C., is a cylindrical mausoleum
that played the role of fortress in
the Middle Ages. It is decorated
below the dripstone by a frieze of
ox skulls.

land at Gaeta. The tower is 30 meters in diameter to 13 meters in height. A circular
passage links four burial chambers arranged on a centripetal plan.

The tall or "pinnacle" tombs are an original formula. The first known example is
situated at Dougga in Tunisia (second century B.C.), of a Punico-Roman design. It
consists of three superimposed square blocks, crowned by a pyramid. A similar
formula exists in the Augustan mausoleum of the Julii (10 B.C.) at Saint Rémy, in
Provence. On a square base, covered in reliefs, stands a tetrapylon formed by
vaulted arches with Corinthian columns at each corner. Above, a light circular
colonnaded lantern, serving as a canopy, completes the design.

La Conocchia of Capua, dating from the first century A.D., is a stonework building that follows more or less the same formula: a square base, a second level consisting of pedimental facades between thick columns at the corners, and a summit
in the form of a *tholos* with embedded columns.

The imagination of the builders of funerary monuments fed off different
sources. The pyramid of Cestius in Rome (18–12 B.C.) reflects the campaign of
Mark Antony and Caesar in Egypt. The tomb of Eurysaces, by the Porta Maggiore
(a later Claudian building), is modeled on the design of a baker's oven of the first
century B.C., not to mention the underground *columbarium* tombs, such as those
at Serviglia, near Carmona in Spain.

All of these examples show that funerary architecture was an important element of Roman commemorative art.

Both the circular and pinnacle categories of tomb display the same subdivision
into three levels: a square ground level, symbolizing the terrestrial world where
the shallow-relief ornamentation represents the actions of the deceased; a second level, which can be square or circular or even cruciform, with concave sur-
faces, in the form of a miniature temple furnished with blind bays, symbolizing,
according to Gilbert Picard, the gateway to hell, the entrance to the other world;
and finally the last level, often circular, in the form of a *tholos* or small temple covered by a conical or pyramidal roof. Picard calls this last level the "sanctuary of the
dead man deified and the symbolic representation of the celestial world in which
he lives for all eternity."

"Pinnacle" Tombs
Page 65 bottom left
In Tunisia the mausoleum tower of
Dougga (Thugga), composed of
three cubes on stepped podiums,
reaches a height of 21 meters at
the top of the pyramid. This Punic
structure was built in the middle
of the second century B.C. by a
strongly Romanized architect.
Page 65 bottom center
La Conocchia of Capua, from the
end of the first century A.D., also
consists of three superposed enti-
ties, with the top circular element
playing the role of *tholos*.
Page 65 bottom right
18 meters in height, the Mausoleum of the Julii at Glanum, near
St. Rémy, similarly decorated with
a *tholos*, was dedicated to the sons
of Agrippa, Caius, and Lucius, and
dates from 10 B.C.

From utilitarian to symbolic

Top left

In Rome, the tomb of Eurysaces pre-dates the construction of the Porta Maggiore bearing the aqueduct Aqua Claudia, in front of which it stands today. It reproduced the shape of the ovens of its owner's bakery business.

Top right

Also in the form of a pyramid, the tomb of Caius Cestius at the Porta San Paolo. It was built in 18-12 B.C.

Center left

The mausoleum of Tipasa (Algeria) is an enormous circular stone tumulus surrounded by a cylindrical substructure punctuated by embedded columns.

Center right

In Rome, the circular structure of the Mausoleum of Augustus, which reaches a diameter of 87 meters once attained 44.5 meters in height.

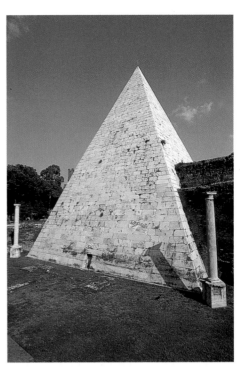

The Rise of the Roman Empire

From Tiberius to Domitian

Augustus's refusal to give free rein to imperial splendor in Rome, combined with the reactionary effect of the theories of Vitruvius, resulted in freezing architectural progress during the Augustan period, both spatially and technologically. A new era began when the emperor died in A.D. 14, at the age of 76. Augustus's long, peaceful reign, extending over 40 years, meant that imperial power, now firmly established, no longer needed to fear expressing the absolutist character of the imperial system.

The Stagecraft of Tiberius's Grotto

Augustus's successor, Tiberius, who reigned from A.D. 14 to 37, displayed a pronounced taste for riches and splendor. The palace of Capri, where he retired in A.D. 26, was, according to the ancients, exceptionally luxurious. Indeed its name, Palace of the Twelve Gods and Villa Jovis (House of Jupiter), showed that the emperor clearly identified himself with the leader of the gods.

Another example illustrates this taste for luxury: the grotto of Tiberius at Sperlonga. In 1957 a systematic excavation of the site revealed an extraordinary focal point where architecture fused with nature, sea with land, and entertainment with religious worship. Tiberius's grotto was a nymphaeum where Odyssean "mysteries" were performed before the emperor, as the traces of remarkable sculpted marble groups that have been uncovered show. One group, set in a semicircle at the back of the cave, showed Ulysses and his companions blinding the giant Polyphemus recumbent on the ground. The other group showed Ulysses on the prow of his ship, while Scylla (a female sea monster who with Charybdis guarded the straits of Messina) seized six of his companions. This group stood on a little island in the center of the cave. All of these marble statues, signed by the Rhodians Agesandros, Polydoros, and Athenadoros, sculptors of the famous Laocoon, were copies of Greek bronzes.

The remarkable feature here is the architectural and geological environment formed by the imperial grotto. The general configuration was achieved by a clever combination of nature and artifice. The interior of the grotto was modified to give it a circular form 22 meters in diameter; the surround of the pool that occupied the center was carved out of the rock itself. The Scylla group stood on a central islet and the Polyphemus group at the back of the grotto, in front of a natural cavity. Seats carved out of the rock on either side of the entrance were intended for spectators. Another cavity on the left consisted of a circular chamber, followed by a cruciform apse.

The central pool was covered by the rocky roof of the cave, left in its natural state by the architect. It was, in fact, from this natural ceiling that a block of stone detached itself during a ceremony, narrowly missing Tiberius, who was saved from death by Sejanus, the prefect of the praetorium. The central pool was connected to an installation built in the sea on the same axis, forming a rectangle 30 meters long and the same width as the circular pool. Forming a rectangular dike, the structure encompassed a second structure, 16 by 8 meters, made up of two parts: on the cave side, a square islet where a portico with "canopy" stood over a tiny "lake"; on the other side, a group of four equally sized tanks, where fish probably swam. These installations, which communicated with the sea, formed an unusual setting for court rituals. The performances, no doubt attended by the emperor and his retinue, probably required mechanical contrivances to produce the apparitions. This veritable *deus ex machina*, consisting of effects including torches, artificial mists, music, and sound, represented the triumph of the individual over his surroundings and over adversity, as personified by Ulysses, the epitome of the hero, model of virtue and courage, who, leading his men and surviving the most terrible of trials, overcame the forces of nature. The mythical spectacle symbolized the hero's apotheosis, a deification process with which the emperor identified.

The structure of this emblematic theater also lent itself to the prediction of the future. At the entrance of the grotto, the four fish aquariums were used for ichthyomancy, (divination based on the color, movements, and speed of the fish observed). This method of predicting the future probably played an important role in Rome, as did astrology and other soothsaying techniques practiced by the augurs who studied the flight of birds (ornithomancy) or by the haruspices who examined the liver of sacrificial victims (hieroscopy). Bernard Andreae states that the Polyphemus grottoes were also built by the emperors Claudius, Nero, and Domitian. Thus, the example at Sperlonga is not unique.

The architectural significance of this extraordinary mechanical arrangement lies in the overall design, formed by a circular element (here covered by a natural vault) to which a rectangular element of the same width was attached. This arrangement in "writing tablet form," to use Varro's expression, was a constant feature already present in the configuration of Pompey's theater and one to which we shall return when considering the so-called Teatro Marittimo of Hadrian at Tivoli and its model, the aviary of the villa of Casinum.

Art and nature
General view of the grotto at Sperlonga. In the foreground are the aquatic installations forming aquariums intended for the practice of ichthyomancy.

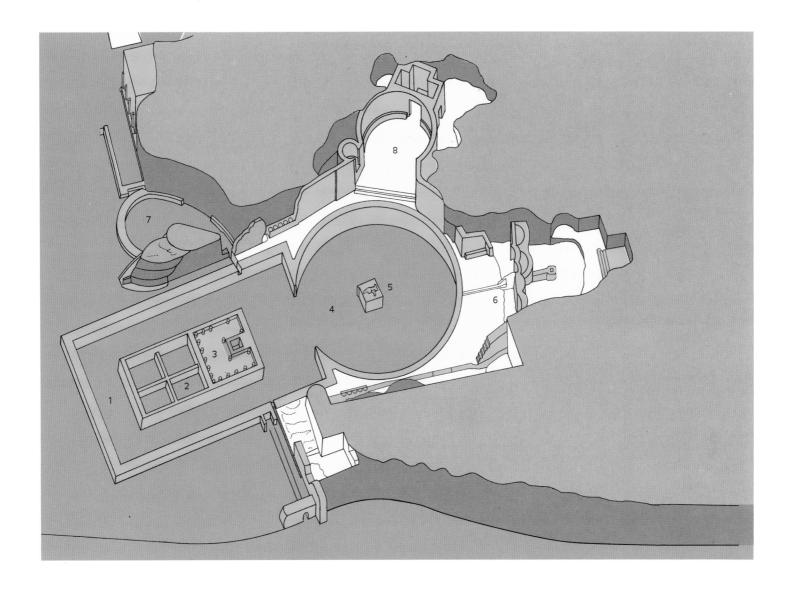

Axonometric view of the grotto at Sperlonga

Tiberius had this grotto created at the beginning of the first century A.D.

1. Artificial pool
2. Aquariums for the purpose of ichthyomancy
3. Pavilion with small coupled columns representing the imperial canopy
4. Circular pool under the vault of rock
5. Islet on which the Scylla sculpture group stood
6. Principal natural cavity containing the Polyphemus group
7. Secondary pool
8. Secondary natural cavity

Nero's Revolutionary Projects

After Tiberius, the reigns of Caligula (A.D. 37–41) and Claudius (A.D. 41–54) were characterized by technical improvements achieved through the utilitarian creations of the first century B.C. It was during the controversial principate of Nero that a true architectural revolution came about, based on the realization of increasingly ambitious works, whose vaults and domes were constructed out of solid concrete.

The creation of major internal spaces had begun less than 60 years before at Baiae, the large thermal establishment near Naples. There, the domed chamber known as the Temple of Mercury, slightly predating the imperial period, consisted of a vast circular space, 21.5 meters in diameter. This dome was constructed in blocks of tufa by means of voussoirs placed in a radial arrangement. The interior was lit by a central *oculus*. This structure, far from being a temple, was part of the thermal building, now partially flooded as a result of the gradual geological collapse of the area caused by chronic volcanic instability. This affected both the southeast of the bay of Naples, as well as the west, including the famous Campi Phlegraeae and Solfatara of Pozzuoli, neighbor of Baiae.

During Nero's reign (A.D. 54–68), the architectural advances and urban transformation of Rome were favored, if such a term is appropriate, by the terrible fire in A.D. 64 that afflicted most districts of the capital, destroying temples, palaces, official buildings, public baths, and private dwellings. Nero – alleged by some ancient writers to have started the fire himself, though there is no evidence to support this – was to make the most of this tragic event. He decreed a series of

Baiae, Roman thermal baths
At the foot of the terraced slopes of the site at Baiae, near Naples, the dome of the Temple of Mercury forms the central element of a thermal establishment.

Domed hall of the Temple of Mercury
Interior view of the domed hall of the Temple of Mercury at Baiae, built around 40 B.C. In addition to the central *oculus*, the sides of this voussoired tufa vault contain square bays open to the outside. As a result of the gradual subsidence of the whole volcanic region, the building is now partly submerged in water.

Water supply and traffic management
The Porta Maggiore in Rome, which carries the aqueducts of Claudius (the Aqua Claudia and the Anio Novus), was finished in A.D. 52. The two arches that allow the circulation of city traffic are flanked by pedimented bays enclosed by embedded columns built in rusticated stone. In the foreground on the right is the tomb of Eurysaces.

regulations regarding the width of streets, the height of dwellings and construction materials used in order to avoid such a disaster in future.

In the center of the ravaged capital, he commandeered approximately 50 hectares stretching from the Palatine hill to the slopes of the Oppian hill on the Esquiline. This zone, where he was to build his palace, included the site where he had begun to build the Domus Transitoria, partially destroyed during the great fire. The vestibule of this building, whose name evoked a "transition," forming as it did a link between the Domus Tiberiana on the Palatine and the gardens of Maecenas on the Esquiline – was built on a cruciform plan. A cupola covered the octagon at the crossing of the four barrel-vaulted corridors. Screens formed by four columns placed across each corridor created lumininous effects in the cruciform interior.

These same features, vast halls without clear limits, are present in the nymphaeum of this palace, with its "wall of water": flowing down the steps of a staircase, the water divided up into a multitude of murmuring cascades that flowed between the columns of a fountain built beneath a portico enclosing a courtyard.

Nero's "astronomical" hall

The Domus Aurea, or the Golden House, is the palace that Nero had built after the fire that ravaged Rome in 64 A.D. The domed hall, called the *coenatio rotunda*, or Octagon Room, is a hemispherical structure built in concrete, 14 meters in diameter, lit from an *oculus* in the center of the dome. On the inside, the architects Severus and Celer fitted spherical elements in wood, creating a "stage decor" that revolved on itself, copying the movement of the stars in the celestial vault.

The splendor of the Palatine buildings

Detail of a floor mosaic discovered in the Domus Tiberiana, on the Palatine, dating from the first half of the first century A.D. The colored marble and the refinement of the design indicate the ostentatious luxury of the imperial palace. (Antiquario Palatino, Rome)

A technological revolution
From an architectural point of view, the dome of Nero's Domus Aurea was innovative by its use – to support the hemispherical roof – of simple pillars situated at the angles of the octagon. Between these supports are square bays with flat horizontal border lintels. Their architraves form the load-bearing element of the dome, inside which the revolving mechanism was fitted.

An "Ecological" Vision

After the great fire of Rome, Nero started the project for the emperor's new palace from scratch. He entrusted the plans for the building to the architects Severus and Celer, who devised an original and surprising scheme: a large parkland with groves of trees planted in the open areas left by the ravages of the fire. Far from erecting a group of vast palatial buildings on a gridlike pattern, the operation consisted of creating, in central Rome, a luxuriant garden with an artificial lake in the middle (in the hollow where the Colosseum was later built).

This scheme, which in modern terminology could be described as ecological, consisted of green spaces planted with exotic tree species, where porticoes, pavilions, arbors, summerhouses, sanctuaries, and fountains were scattered. The Arcadian atmosphere evoked the Hellenistic-style frescoes that were being painted in the same period in Pompeii. This landscape gardening reflected the different realms of the universe: does and stags frolicked there; birds sang in the huge aviaries; fishes with gold and silver scales thrived in the brimming sparkling pools.

The whole formed a veritable Garden of Eden, in the image of the gardens created long before by the Achemenids of Persia, then by the Parthians and the Hellenistic rulers, a *paradeisos*, where the many species of nature are present, the whole stamped with the omnipotence of a *cosmocrator*.

The palatial complex covered the slopes of the Oppian hill, overlooking this marvelous parkland at the entrance of which stood a colossal statue 36 meters high depicting the emperor as a sun god. Facing south, the facade of the palace,

Persian sun cult
In Nero's time, the Persian cult of Mithras, involving the sacrifice of a bull to the sun god, spread throughout the Empire. This fresco of the Mithraeum of Capua, which dates from the second century A.D. illustrates the gesture of the priest, coiffed with a Phrygian bonnet, at the moment of sacrifice.

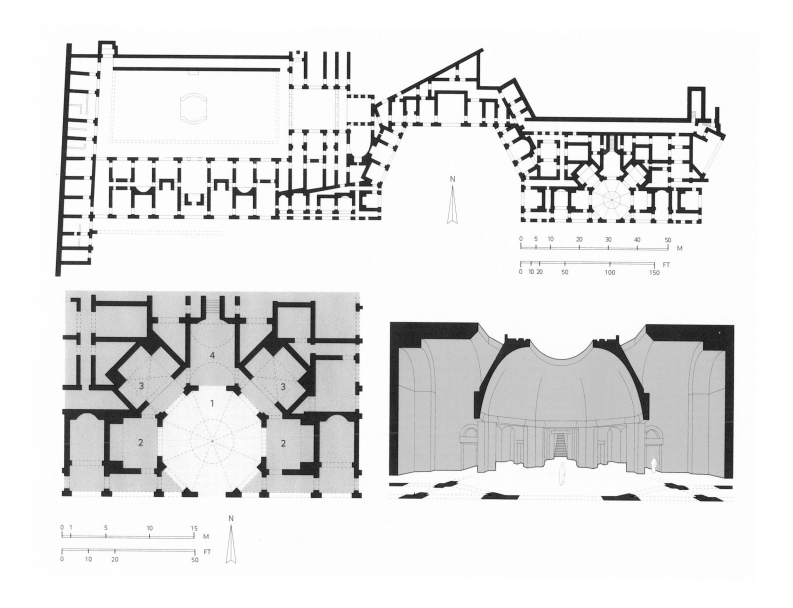

Nero's Palace

Top
Plan of the Domus Aurea, or palace of Nero. The central part forms a large exedra, which separates the private apartments (on the left) from the hall reserved for court ritual or *coenatio rotunda* (on the right).

Bottom left: detail of the Octagon Room:
1. The Rotunda
2. The alcove rooms
3. The *triclinia*
4. The nymphaeum and waterfall

Bottom right: Section through the rotunda and its connecting rooms.

called the Domus Aurea, was approximately 260 meters wide. The center consisted of a huge exedra, 50 meters wide, in the shape of a semioctagon. This unusual design recalls the large *iwans* of Persia where the Parthian rulers sat enthroned to receive their worshipping subjects.

The name of Nero's palace (Domus Aurea) derives from the profusion of gold decor that covered its walls. Instead of the black and red walls common in Pompeii and Herculaneum, Nero chose to use luminous colors in reflective materials, particularly gold, symbolizing the sun, for he wished to identify himself with the sun. He assumed the characteristics of a syncretic deity combining Apollo, Helios and Mithra – a mixture of Hellenistic, Armenian and Parthian elements.

The Logistics of the Domus Aurea

In the eastern wing of the Domus Aurea, Nero commissioned his architect-engineers Severus and Celer to build an octagonal chamber. This was a *coenatio* (salon-dining room) with a hemispherical cupola 14 meters in diameter. This octagon, lit from a central *oculus,* was surrounded by a peripheral corridor that consisted of a series of interconnecting rooms. In addition to the two lateral rooms with alcoves were two *triclinia* placed on the diagonal axes, on either side of a central vaulted nymphaeum, at the back of which water poured down a stepped cascade.

This domed chamber was built of concrete, the fruit of revolutionary technology. Its square doorways, surmounted by a brick lintel, directly supported the solid concrete dome. Such a formula was completely modern. This *coenatio* also

included a remarkable feature designed to reflect the prowess of the architects and technicians, "whose bold imagination and skilled craftsmanship enabled them to achieve all that the emperor desired and nature could not provide." (Tacitus, 42). Regarding this *coenatio*, Suetonius wrote: "The main chamber was round and revolved continually day and night, as does the world" (Nero, 31). "The ceiling," he noted, "was made of ivory marquetery with movable panels from which flower petals and perfume could be showered on the guests." Seneca, who had been Nero's preceptor, specified (*Letter to Lucilius*, Book XIV, 90, 14) that "a technician invented a system by which saffron-colored water poured down from a great height and also succeeded in assembling the panels of this chamber's ceiling in such a way that its appearance changed at will." What could this have been?

Despite the *damnatio memoriae* that was supposed to eradicate Nero's memory, archaeologists found the remains of this curious building preserved beneath Trajan's baths that covered over the famous Domus Aurea after the emperor's suicide. The chamber was well preserved, and, around the *oculus*, two grooves serving as rails can be seen. These rails were used to suspend rotating semispherical painted wooden panels that conformed to the shape of the cupola's interior. These concentric elements made of marquetry, fitted with panels and openings, could thus revolve at different speeds, "as does the universe," with the "luminaries" (the sun and moon) appearing.

Given our knowledge of the importance of astral phenomena in the worship of Mithras, who was considered the master of the constellations and the zodiac, it

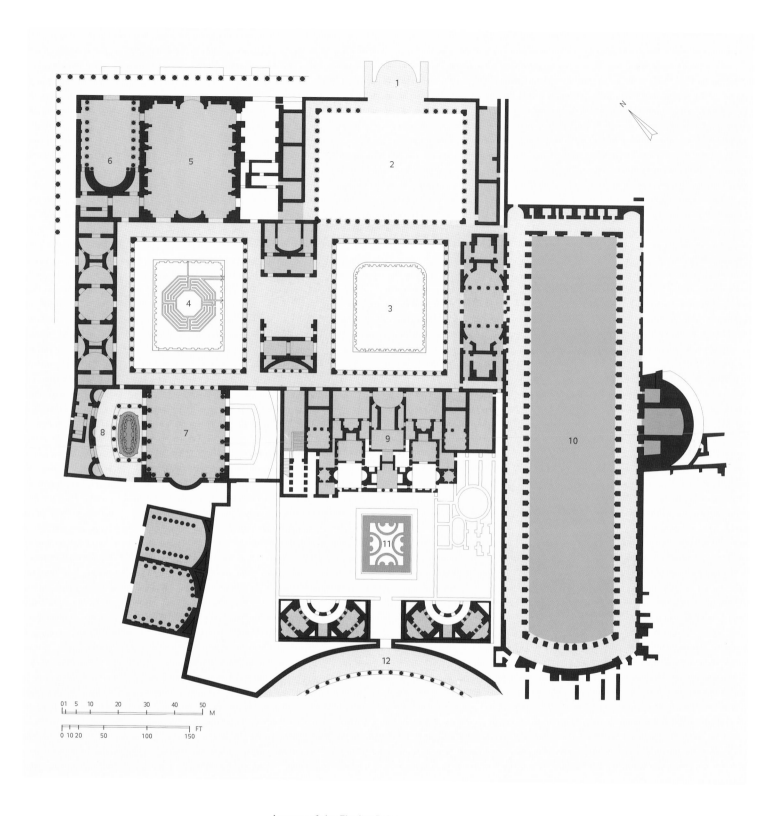

Layout of the Flavian Palace

Plan of the Domus Flavia on the Palatine in Rome. This palace, built by Domitian between A.D. 80 and 92 by the architect Rabirius, covers 5 hectares.

1. Propylaeum or entrance
2. First peristyle courtyard
3. Second peristyle courtyard
4. Third peristyle courtyard with labyrinth
5. *Aula regia*, or throne room
6. Basilical hall
7. *Triclinium* of the *coenatio Jovis* (dining room of Jupiter)
8. Nymphaeum
9. Domus Augustana, or private apartments (detail page 80)
10. Stadium-hippodrome with surrounding portico
11. Fountain and peristyle
12. Large *exedra* overlooking the Circus Maximus

becomes obvious that the mechanism, which never stopped moving "night or day" in Nero's "Palace of the Sun," aimed to recreate in visual terms the planetary movements (*imago mundi*) and suggest the progress of the stars in the heavens. Similarly, the role of the pipes (*fistulae*), which allowed water to sprinkle onto the guests, was to demonstrate the power that the deified sovereign possessed over rain, an essential element of the ritual of the *hieros gamos* (sacred marriage uniting heaven and earth). In a setting as sophisticated as this, a *deus ex machina* was employed to express the omnipotence of the emperor.

Given the technological and mechanical knowledge that the ancients had at their disposal, the method by which Severus and Celer managed to create such wonders is a question that we shall consider in connection with Hadrian's palace at Tivoli. It should be pointed out straightaway, however, that such creations, albeit rare, were already known in Rome at the time of the Republican author Terentius Varro (116–27 B.C.). These mechanisms were related to cosmological symbolism and to astrological practices involving the consultation of the horoscope.

The Domus Flavia of Domitian

The Flavian dynasty succeeded the now-dishonored and despised Nero, whose palace would be buried in the basements of Trajan's baths (98–117). This new dynasty decided to replace the Domus Aurea with a palace that would reflect its own power. It would be built on the Palatine hill, regaining its original position. The Palatine hill (from which the word palace derives) was the most important of the "seven hills" of Rome and formed the center of the prehistoric *vicu*. During the Republican era, a number of religious buildings were built there. Augustus had

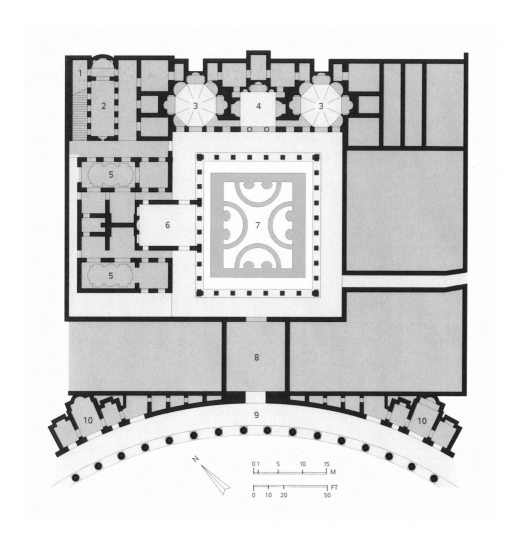

Imperial palace on the Palatine
Plan of the private quarters of the palace, or the Domus Augustana, on the Palatine, Rome:
 1. Stairways to the lower floor
 2. Apsidal nymphaeum
 3. Octagonal vaulted chambers
 4. Room with three apses
 5. Rooms with fountains
 6. Large *triclinium* overlooking garden
 7. Interior garden with peristyle and fountain
 8. Vaulted vestibule
 9. Large exedra overlooking the Circus Maximus
10. Boudoirs

The Materials and Methods of Roman Building

The *opus reticulatum* of a wall in Ostia

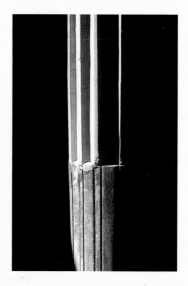

Detail of a fluted column in stucco from Stabia

The development of Roman architecture was dictated by the need for large chambers and vast covered halls for civic, commercial, and religious purposes. These requirements resulted in the creation of ever-larger internal spaces with increasingly bold and imaginative solutions for the vaults that covered them.

The advances were based first and foremost on a perfect stonecutting technique, ranging from the early polygonal walls to creations built in large, squared blocks. They are based in particular on the knowledge of stereotomy (the art of stonecutting) applied to arch voussoirs and vaults, before being applied to stone cupolas. The Romans were grand masters of building in large blocks assembled without mortar or with a liquid mortar that aided waterproofing. They generally used metal cramp-irons (of iron or bronze) to ensure the cohesion of the structures.

Side by side with this art of cut stone, the use of brick emerged at the beginning of the Empire (under Tiberius). Brick was known well before that date, but it was used in monumental architecture and official buildings only in the supporting structures and roofs when it was possible to hide its basic appearance with marble ornamentation. In general brick was reserved for utilitarian buildings: shops, *insulae*, industrial buildings, and workshops. But brick structures with marble facings, conferring an appearance of luxury and pomp, were increasingly used for the most sumptuous and prestigious imperial temples and palaces. A brick structure presented considerable advantages over stone: it was lighter, more supple, and easier to work. In addition, the facing concealed the diverse materials used for practical reasons: stone foundations, brick walls, and roofs in tufa or travertine. By this technique, a varied masonry was given an appearance of unity.

Buildings with no official or ceremonial capacity had a layer of stucco that replaced the facing or cladding marble. This system had already been used to decorate Greek monuments and conceal lesser-quality stone, used in regions that did not have marble quarries. The stucco covering of columns and walls, commonly seen in Pompeii, was widely used in private homes.

Stucco was also used as sculpted decoration. Certain sumptuous residences in Rome, such as the villa discovered under the Farnesina (19 B.C.) and the underground basilica at the Porta Maggiore (middle of the first century A.D.), have elaborate ornamentation in stucco shallow relief.

The main technological revolution of western Roman architecture lies in the use of solid concrete, obtained by mixing mortar with *pozzolona*, consisting of gravel and brick fragments. The advantage of this material was that it could be "poured" into wooden molds, enabling the realization of what amounts to monolithic vaults and cupolas.

The novelty of concrete was stressed when the sanctuary of Fortuna at Palestrina was discussed. The importance of coffering should also be underlined. This technique permitted the creation of circular coffered vaults, permitting the structure to be made lighter without weakening it. This revolution of concrete enabled the creation of free, sweeping spaces. The Domus Aurea was an eloquent example; its octagonal hall, diagonal spaces, and wide horizontal sweeps, where wedge-shaped bricks appear in straight layers, free the architect from the tyranny of arches at the base of a dome.

The diverse types of wall construction techniques had the following Latin names: the *opus quadratum*, large, squared stones laid in horizontal courses; the *opus incertum*, or facing of concrete achieved with irregular small blocks of stone; the *opus reticulatum*, like the *opus incertum* but forming on the visible area a network of regular polygonal blocks; the *opus latericium*, or masonry of brick; the *opus testaceum*, or core of concrete faced with fired brick. The *opus caementarium* refers to ashlar work, whereas the *opus caementicium* refers to cement block foundation, which permitted the development of vaults and domes created by means of a thin layer, achieved by means of coffering.

Roman architects and engineers had at their disposal a large repertoire of materials that they employed to achieve a complex syntax, endowed with many technological formulas permitting the creation of curvilinear elements, such as the arch, the vault, and the dome.

lived there in a relatively simple house, belonging to his wife, Livia, and standing among the aristocratic residences. Tiberius built the first imperial palace there, the Domus Tiberiana. Because the remains lie beneath the Farnese gardens, it has not been possible to carry out any extensive excavations, but according to recent research, Tiberius's palace consisted of a complex measuring 400 by 450 feet (117.6 by 132.3 meters), on a rigorously geometrical design. The area was subdivided into six squares, each measuring 150 feet. In the center was a cryptoporticus, 100 by 150 feet. These measurements show the importance that even numbers held for the Romans, to which they probably ascribed particular significance. The remains of the palace are being studied by Clemens Krause and a team of archaeologists; their excavations show great promise.

Domitian built his Domus Flavia on the Palatine, a huge imperial complex designed to bolster his autocratic power. Occupying the western side of the hill, impressive remains several stories high have been uncovered. They consist of a series of ceremonial courtyards surrounded by peristyles and, situated to the north, a grandiose throne room once covered by a barrel vault with a span of 32 meters, designed by the architect Rabirius. On the east side of the palace was a small-scale replica of a stadium-hippodrome, 160 by 50 meters, surrounded by a peristyle. Situated on a north-west-southeast axis, it included a semicircular box for the emperor, in the middle of its southern portico.

Behind the large *exedra* overlooking the Circus Maximus, stood the private palace of the emperor, known as the Domus Augustana. The two-story palace contained the private quarters of the prince, composed of complex vaulted chambers with *triclinium*, arranged around a columned courtyard-nymphaeum.

19th century miniature mosaic depicting the Roman Forum
On the left, in front of the dome of the church of Saints Luca and Martina, stands the Arch of Septimius Severus. In the centre, the eight columns of the facade of the Temple of Saturn. On the right, the three columns of the Temple of Castor and Pollux in front of Santa Maria Antiqua.

Ornament in the imperial gardens
Detail of the oval nymphaeum on a mixtilinear plan (alternance of straight and curved lines) in the Domus Flavia. This "island" in the center of an oval pool illustrates the tendency toward baroque design that emerges from Domitian's time.

Stadium-hippodrome
View of the stadium-hippodrome situated on the eastern side of the Domus Flavia and the Domus Augustana. Traces of the two-story peristyle are visible. On the left stands the building that housed the imperial tribunal (*cathisma*), where the emperor watched the entertainments over which he presided.

A colossal construction for the people

The Flavian amphitheater, or Colosseum, built from A.D. 70, comprises three stories of arcades and a blind attic story that reach a height of 50 meters. Each story consists of 80 arches. Embedded columns punctuate the facade: the first story is in Tuscan style, the second in Ionic, and the third Corinthian. The huge *velum* that sheltered the *cavea* was attached to masts that projected from the top of the building.

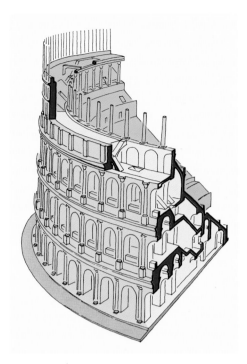

Axonometric view of the Colosseum
The cutaway axonometric view of the Colosseum shows the arrangement of the internal structures and the passgeways under the seating of the *cavea*.

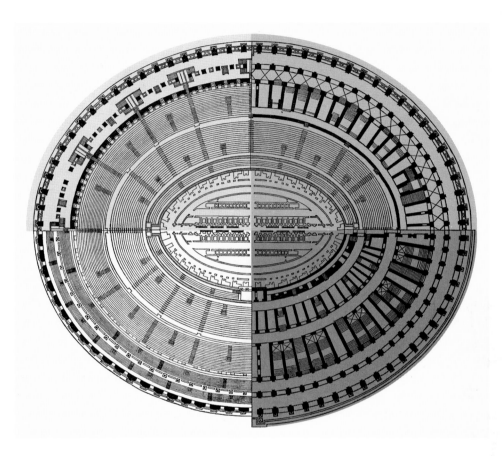

Right
Ellipse of stone
The plan of the Flavian amphitheater, a huge construction built in travertine, forms an oval of 188 by 156 meters. Because of this oval form, each quarter of the building is composed of arches, galleries, and vaults that all have a slightly different shape, a fact that must have posed complicated problems of stereotomy.

The *aula regia* in the *sanctum palatium*

The throne room, built by Rabirius between A.D. 80 and 92, was 45 by 32 meters, an area of 1440 square meters without any intermediate support. Inside, the projecting piers of the tranverse ribs, designed to support the barrel vault, punctuated the flatness of the walls, forming a series of decorative bays. This hall was reserved for the ceremony of *proskynesis* (prostration before the sovereign). It thus performed the function of a public audience chamber, one of the traditional features of the official palace, in contrast to the hall for private audiences, intended for the assembly of the imperial council. The latter, built with a basilical apse decorated with columns, stood to the west of the *aula regia*. To the south was a garden-courtyard surrounded by a portico. The ground was covered by an octagonal labyrinthine mosaic. This area lay before a splendid chamber containing the imperial *triclinium*. This *coenatio Jovis* (or Dining Hall of Jupiter), as it was called, was the sacred place where the emperor appeared in majesty during certain ceremonial court rituals in his sacred palace (*sanctum palatium*).

The ceremonial hall, 29 by 33 meters, caused much ink to flow, even during the emperor's own lifetime. The poets Statius and Martial described the "*tholos* of Caesar" that stood there, a canopy-*ciborium* of sorts, acting as the stage for apparitions. Domitian would appear there in the role of a god – as Nero did in the *coenatio* of the Domus Aurea. Statius adds that the canopy beneath which the imperial throne was placed was decorated with "stars like those of the celestial vault" (*astra polumque*). This hall thus also contained an image of the cosmos

Panem et circences:
Bread and Circus Games
The huge *cavea* of the Colosseum
could accommodate around
70 000 spectators who came to
see gladiatorial duels, combat
with lions and other wild beasts,
and sea battles (initially the arena
could be flooded to form a pool
intended for naval jousts). Underground modifications later provided menageries, and changing
rooms for the combatants. They
also contained the mechanisms
of the stage sets for the lion hunt
and battles. Today, the absence of
most of the seating that accom-
modated the Roman crowds calls
for a mental reconstruction of the
immense conical and oval space
that greeted the spectators in the
Flavian amphitheater.

Page 88

Amphitheater of Pozzuoli
In the amphitheater of Pozzuoli, near Naples (149 by 116 meters), contemporary with the Colosseum in Rome, the corridors and the infrastructure consist of brick arches and concrete vaulting. They offer an opportunity to study the arrangements for the movement of people under the rows of seating as well as the amenities intended for the lions under the arena.

The oval arena of Capua
In the town of Capua, famous for its *"delizie"* and its circus games, traces survive of the large amphitheater (167 by 137 meters) dating from the first century A.D. Only the arena of this vast construction remains visible. Its three stories of arcades have completely disappeared since its masonry was used rather like a quarry by medieval populations.

(*imago mundi*). Its cosmic nature was underscored in a poem in which Martial addressed the architect himself: "Oh Rabirius, you, whose marvelous skill is building the imperial home on the hill of Evander (the Palatine), you have created there the sky and its stars with your piously devoted spirit" (*Epigrams*, VII, 56). Likewise, in the *Silvae* Statius stresses the fact that, on entering the palace he "found himself with Jupiter (Domitian himself) amongst the stars." Apparently there existed at the Flavian palace, a sort of planetarium, similar to that at the Domus Aurea, where Domitian displayed his absolute power over the terrestrial and astral universes.

At the same time as the emperor was commissioning Rabirius to construct the Domus Flavia, he also had to deal with the consequences of a new fire that ravaged Rome for three days and three nights in A.D. 80. The Capitol in particular was destroyed and had to be rebuilt without delay. As Nero had before him, so Domitian took legal measures to protect the town, forbidding the proliferation of shops at the foot of *insulae*, in order to avoid the spread of fire. He also decided to

restore the importance of Rome's libraries, twice devastated by the fires of 64 and 80, and sent copyists all the way to Alexandria. In the forum, Domitian built a temple dedicated to his father, Vespasian, and erected the arch of Titus to commemorate the capture of Jerusalem and the sacking of the Temple of the Jews. He also built the temple of Isis and Serapis in the Campus Martius, heralding the penetration of Asian religions in the capital. Like Nero, Domitian was a despotic persecutor of Christians resistant to the imperial religion who met a dramatic end at the hands of assassins. And like Nero too, his name was to be the object of a *damnatio memoriae*, condemned to be forgotten.

A Gigantic Creation: The Colosseum

It was under Vespasian (69–79) that the Flavian amphitheater, or Colosseum, was built, with its inauguration taking place during Titus's reign, in A.D. 80. This gigantic building, designed for circus entertainments and built on the remains of the gardens Nero had created around his palace, occupied the spot where the

artificial lake had been situated in front of the Domus Aurea. Building started in 70 and lasted approximately a decade. The elliptical arena, intended for official ceremonies and for spectacles where gladiators pitted their strength against wild animals, recalls a Campanian, or, more precisely, Samnite model. In Italy, the oldest known example exists at Pompeii, built in the time of Sulla. In Rome, the first amphitheater dates from 29 B.C.

An amphitheater could be perceived as the combination of two theaters with opposing *caveas* forming a circular space. However, the absence of a stage wall represents an important difference between these two types of public building. Furthermore, the ellipsoidal plan of the amphitheater differs from the semi-circular shape of the theater. The creation of these stone amphitheaters is therefore related to that of theaters only by certain architectural elements, such as the rows of seating, exterior arcading, vaulted corridors, and access stairways. The construction of amphitheaters, with their circular passageways and sloping barrel-vaulted ramps, posed considerable problems of stereotomy due to the total lack of right angles, a problem that the Roman architects tackled impressively.

The plan of the Colosseum, the largest amphitheater of the Empire, reached 188 meters at its longest point and 156 meters at its widest. The three stories of stone arcades up to the cornice rise to almost 50 meters. The facade of this grandiose monument, totaling 80 arcades on three levels, features a design where the different Doric, Ionic, and Corinthian orders are superimposed. This arrangement had been used since Hellenistic times and was to have as great an importance in ancient architecure as in Renaissance architecture. Travertine was used on the outside, and stucco, decorated in polychrome relief sculpture, covered some of the corridors. Some traces survive today. A circle of statues stood silhouetted against the sky on the top cornice.

Toward the afterlife
A touching scene from the *mithraeum* of Capua: an "angel" with butterfly wings leads toward the Elysian Fields the soul of a deceased man, represented as a childlike winged figure.

Page 90 top
Massive vaulting
View through the impressive brick vaults of the infrastructure of Capua's amphitheater. In its remarkably preserved underground areas, one can see the organization of the technical department under the arena of the building designed for popular entertainments.

A theater in Britain
In Britain, where the implantation of Roman civilization begun by Caesar reached its peak during Hadrian's reign, buildings intended for entertainment also played an important role. A city like Verulamium, near St. Albans, which was destroyed by fire in 155, managed to rise again complete with a large theater of which only traces survive today. The building remained in use up to the fourth century.

The Colosseum could contain some 70 000 spectators. Underground areas were equipped to house wild animals, and water-carrying systems were engineered with the requisite waterproofing, enabling the creation of a pool 80 meters by 54 meters in the arena for the staging of mock sea battles. With great ceremony, the emperor and his entourage sat in the canopied imperial box, a sight that must have conferred a unique ambience to the building dedicated to games and popular celebrations. Huge colored awnings (*velum*) were stretched across the *cavea* by means of a system of ropes, halyards, and rigging, in order to protect the spectators from the sun, for the festivities organized by the authorities, to which the Roman people were summoned, could last several days or even weeks.

The Empire built amphitheaters in all its large urban centers, to symbolize the generosity of the emperor. Capua, Pozzuoli, Verona, Pola, Nîmes, Arles, Italica, and Silchester all contain examples of these prestigious constructions. In every respect, the techniques of construction demonstrate the virtuosity of the masons and stonecutters when confronted by the challenge of a three-dimensional ellipsoidal structure.

The inauguration of the Colosseum in A.D. 80 and the accompanying celebrations over 100 days took place during the reign of Titus. The emperor Vespasian had died just a few months before, after the tragic eruption of Vesuvius had utterly destroyed the sunny cities of Pompeii, Herculaneum and Stabia, suddenly buried under lava, mud, and ash.

THE VANISHED CITIES OF VESUVIUS

Pompeii, Herculaneum and Stabia

Page 93
Flight and fall
This agate cameo from the Farnese collection, of the first century B.C., was found at Pompeii. It depicts Icarus, wings outstretched, standing on an altar. The hero is surrounded by Artemis and Daedalus on the left, and by Pasiphae on the right. Width: 4.4 cm. (Museo Nazionale, Naples)

In the Gulf of Naples on 24 August 79, catastrophe struck the towns situated at the foot of Vesuvius and buried the many inhabitants who had not fled, obliterating monuments, temples, dwellings, and harbors. It was not the first disaster to strike the region: 17 years earlier, in 62, after a long period of relative calm, a tremor had announced the reawakening of the volcano. It had damaged a number of buildings that were still being repaired when the real disaster struck.

During a day that seemed as dark as night, 4 meters of ash fell on Pompeii within the space of a few hours. The day after, only a few superstructures protuded from the ashes, landmarks to the survivors, who tried to retrieve their buried belongings. Later, limeburners and looters stripped away the marble and other precious materials that were visible.

The entire town of Herculaneum, directly below the volcano, was submerged by a huge tide of laval mud that solidified into a compact mass. Its destruction was total; most of its buildings disappeared.

Gradually, however, the fertile region was repopulated, and the tragedy was forgotten, until the eighteenth century. In 1748 Charles III of Spain, king of the Two Sicilies, decided to organize archaeological excavations to enrich the collection of antiques in his palaces. Haphazard exploration was carried out by these enthusiastic visitors who were no better than treasure hunters, looking for objects of curiosity value, with no interest in protecting the monuments or understanding their quite exceptional context.

Johann J. Winckelmann condemned the treasure hunters' carelessness. He understood that, in historical terms, the evidence of the buried buildings was of unparalleled importance. In that place, time had stopped in A.D. 79, and no one, or at least almost no one, had disturbed the order of things that had been frozen by the eruption, to await future discovery. What the buried cities teach us is made all the more fascinating by the fact that, almost 2000 years hence, nothing – no transformations, reuse, invasion or reoccupation – has changed the character of these conurbations; quiet coastal towns whose pleasant climate attracted many visitors, thus swelling the local population.

The Ruins of Pompeii

Vesuvius before the eruption of A.D. 79
Pompeian painting depicting Vesuvius covered in vineyards, with a Bacchus-Dionysus figure represented as a bunch of grapes. He holds a thyrsus and is accompanied by a panther; a snake – a chthonian symbol – protects the home. (Museo Nazionale, Naples)

Today three-fifths of Pompeii has been excavated. The perimeter of the town within the Republican city walls encloses approximately 1 kilometer west-east and 750 meters north-south. From an early date, it was possible to discern the layout of the town, which reflects its double origin. From the sixth century B.C., Greek settlers had established themselves there, building a temple contemporary to those at Paestum. The town next passed temporarily into the hands of the Etruscans, who were hounded out in 474 B.C. Then, Samnite and Oscan tribes settled there, with the Romans subsequently taking over. During the civil wars in 90 B.C., Sulla settled the veterans of his army there after their return from the East. In the oldest part of the town, the layout bears the mark of the Samnite and Oscan

period, with the forum placed in an area developed haphazardly. On the eastern side and to the north of the via Fortuna, Hippodamian influence can be seen in the regular grid of streets that intersect at right angles.

The thoroughfares were meticulously paved with large slabs of trachyte and were designed to drain away rainwater. A clever application of raised stone blocks permitted pedestrians to cross the streets from one pavement to the other without getting thier feet wet. On the street front, shops and refreshment counters (*thermopolia*) alternated with plain expanses of wall and occasionally colonnaded loggias.

The Pompeian House

The exterior walls of the Pompeian house were usually plain. Its internal centripetal organization was based on two elements: a central *atrium* with *compluvium*, beneath which the *impluvium* collected the rainwater. The principal rooms of the house were situated around this area, with light coming in from above.

The second element consisted of an interior garden, often surrounded by a columned portico, which represented the private retreat where the occupants relaxed in the natural green setting. This garden area was surrounded by a peristyle with a group of private rooms sometimes leading from it.

This domestic architecture has a double cultural origin: the atrium is typically Italic, whereas the peristyle is Greek, drawing its inspiration, on a larger scale, from houses on Delos. Many of the prosperous houses of the Pompeian region conformed to this model, which developed in response to specific needs. It resulted from the demands of a walled city where space was relatively restricted. Contrary to a long-held belief, this formula does not represent the typical Roman

Pompeian street design
The paving, in the street of the forum, which becomes the street of Mercury, at Pompeii. An ingenious arrangement of raised blocks in the street allowed pedestrians to cross the roads during strong downpours, without impeding the movement of the wagons. In the background is the so-called arch of Caligula.

Page 97
In the shadow of the volcano
At the foot of Vesuvius's still-menacing outline, the Via Stabiana is lined by a series of private houses excavated before 1865.

house. It was, rather, a solution midway between the patrician villas isolated in the middle of the country and the humbler dwellings of the urban *insulae*, such as those in Rome and Ostia.

This characterization is obviously an oversimplification, since variations in the different types in use during its three centuries are numerous in Pompeii. The *atrium* sometimes had four columns; it was then called a tetrastyle *atrium* (a column at each corner of the *impluvium*). The Corinthian *atrium* (if it consists of a larger number of columns) constituted an intermediary formula between *atrium* and peristyle. In large houses, the *atrium* could even be split into two. The peristyle also varied widely. It sometimes surrounded nothing more than a simple patio or pool, but it could also take the form of a portico surrounding a large garden, with its surface area equal to the rest of the building.

This category of Pompeian house often had only a ground floor; however, its restriction within the urban perimeter did not preclude some examples achieving vast proportions. Some houses, such as that of Loreius Tiburtinus, occupying a whole "block," covered an area, including the garden, of 25 by 75 meters (or more than 1800 square meters).

Outside the city's boundary walls, constructed at the time of the Samnite conflicts, villas were built and could reach a considerable size. This is the case, in particular, to the west of the city, of the villa of Diomedes and the Villa dei Misteri, both dating from the beginning of the imperial period (middle of the first century A.D.). The latter, measuring 60 meters square, covers a surface area of 3600 square meters.

The center of Pompeii
At the northernmost side of the Forum of Pompeii, the arch of Nero stands next to the *macellum* (public market) on the square once surrounded by the marble columns of a portico.

Page 99
A forum excavated in the nineteenth century
Plan of the Forum of Pompeii, according to the 1824 survey of Felix-Emmanuel Callet. To the north is the open area of the forum itself, with the capitol, or the Temple of Jupiter. To the east is the *macellum*, or market square, with its central circular pavilion. Below is the sanctuary of the Lares, then the Temple of Vespasian and the large rectangle of the Building of Eumachia. Opposite, to the west of the forum is the Temple of Apollo, to the south of which stands the basilica.

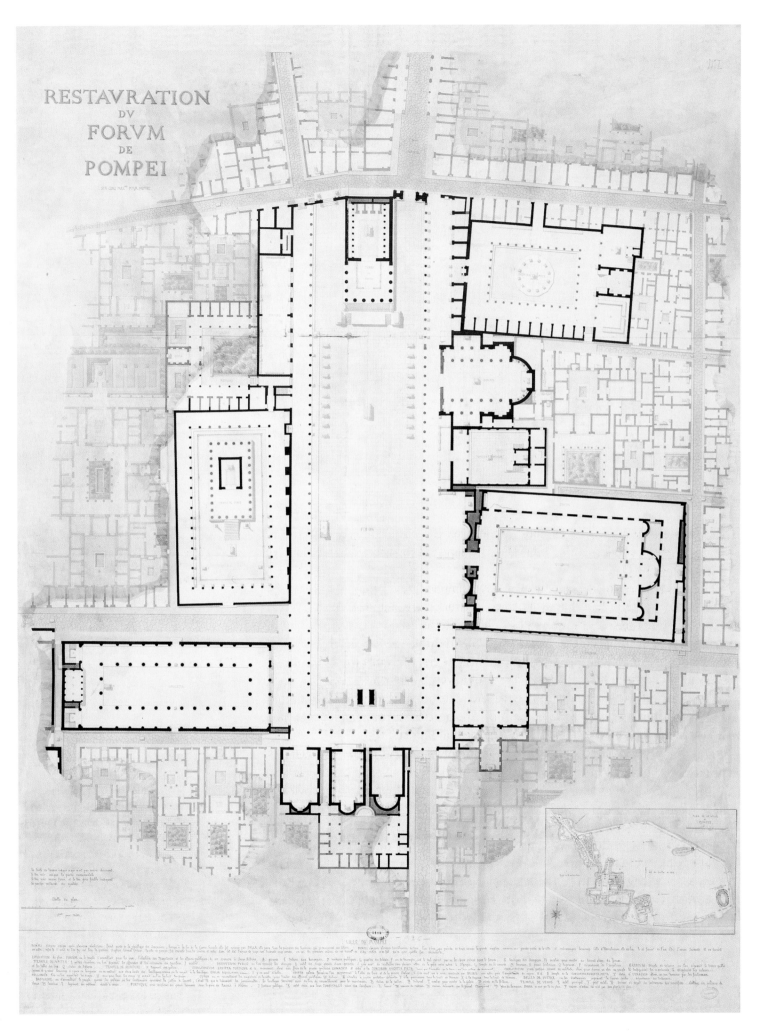

RESTAVRATION
DV
FORVM
DE
POMPEI

The Structure and Decoration of the Private House

Only a few inhabitants of the cities around Vesuvius had enough money to build in marble, apart from certain quarters of the imperial residences, as at Oplontis. Indeed before 79, few private houses were built with the same materials as those used in the construction of temples. Generally the perimeter wall surrounding the house was constructed in rustic masonry. It included tie-irons, lintels, and wooden posts, probably as a precautionary measure against earthquakes, and bore a resemblance to rural half-timbered constructions. The body of the wall was then made in *opus incertum* (with ashlar of various sizes) or in *opus quasi reticulatum* or *reticulatum* (a surface of more or less regular stonework) where the cladding hid the masonry core. These walls also occasionally included tufa or brick anchorage (*opus testaceum*). Brick was also used decoratively, as it was later to be used at Ostia where its continual development can be seen. Sometimes the wooden struc-

A shopping street in Pompeii
A facade overlooking the Via dell'Abondanza, in Pompeii, is composed of a columned loggia over the shops. Homes that open onto the street are rare in Pompeii.

ture favored the development of corbeled upper stories and projecting balconies, as exemplified at Herculaneum.

Fluted columns, either monolithic or in stone sections, were the preserve of the most prestigious buildings; the majority of porticoes consisted of stonework columns, coated, sometimes quite thickly, with a covering that could be polished or fluted, and painted to give the illusion of white or veined marble.

Finally, mention should be made of the role of color in the home, for polychromy played an important part in the everyday context. Inside the house, the walls were always covered with a layer of plaster. This consisted of a first coarse layer, then a more refined surface in fine plaster or stucco, on which the final painted layer was applied. This was sometimes a monochrome surface made up of panels outlined by bands of a different color or a decoration in fresco. A dressed-stone finish could be imitated in stucco, a material allowing the creation of sculpted reliefs that were either chiseled or molded, and then retouched.

Traditionally, the roofing of the Roman house was made of a wooden frame, with its timbers showing, in particular under the *atrium*. The pitch of the ridge-backed roofs was relatively slight, not more than 35 to 45 degrees. The covering tiles were flat or round, the latter arranged with the curve alternately up and down.

Most of the interior fittings – stairs, rails, doors, corridors, partitions, and so on – were in wood. Certain houses had hot-air central heating systems (by hypocaust). At Pompeii, however, heating was usually provided by braziers. Water was supplied in lead pipes with a corresponding drainage system. The most elaborate amenities of the villas were their private baths or thermal installations. In the city, where accommodation was more basic, the citizens used public baths, where the facilities were complex and luxurious, equipped with a changing room (*apodyterium*), a cold room (*frigidarium*), a warm room (*tepidarium*), and a hot room (*caldarium*), in addition to a hot, dry room for steam baths (*laconicum*). These were additional to the bath itself (*alveus*) and the much larger swimming pool (*natatio*).

The Interplay between Interior and Exterior Space

The inhabited space of the Pompeian urban home (*domus pompeiana*) played on a series of contrasts and variations that constitute the originality of this type of building, the contrast of luminosity between the well of light in the atrium and the rooms that surround it. The rooms were usually windowless and received light only through the doorway and the opening formed by the compluvium in the roof, recalling the roof opening over the hearth in the earliest primitive dwellings. Leading off the atrium were the kitchen and the dining room (winter *triclinium*). At meals, the family reclined on wooden benches around a small central table.

Another source of light was the garden surrounded by its portico where the relatively small bedrooms (*cubiculum*) were situated. Between the *atrium* and the peristyle was the *tablinum*, a reception room of sorts. On account of its position and its wide exits leading to the two light areas, its function was mainly transitional, despite the partitions and double doors that could shut it off.

The private area of the home constituted the most interesting spatial arrangement. The presence of a peristyle enabled the rooms and open halls (*exedra*) and even the private sitting room of the master (*oecus*) to be arranged around the garden. The transition from shade to brutal light of day is made in the hallway constituted by this portico. Neither interior nor exterior, this area provided a walkway, sheltered from sun and rain, around the garden, leading to the summer *triclinium* built in stonework, and sometimes covered in marble, where residents dined in the cool during the heat of summer. The role of the *triclinium*, originally a place of familial conviviality, was gradually transformed, through courtly rituals, into a place of "communion" with the deified sovereign.

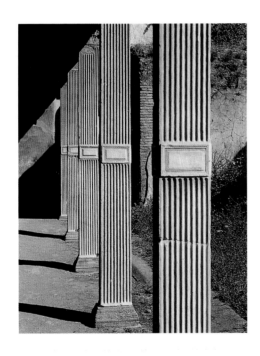

A sumptuous marble portico
Rectangular marble pillars, fluted with Corinthian capitals, forming the portico of the house of Julia Felix at Pompeii.

Page 103
Atrium of the Casa dei Vettii
The vast *atrium* of the house of the Vettii, at Pompeii, leads directly to the peristyle around a fine interior garden. On the edge of the roof, one can note the presence of ceramic gargoyles and acroteria.

Interior of a Vesuvian home
Villa of Stabia with its tetrastyle *atrium* (a column at each corner of the *compluvium*) and its deep *impluvium*. The stucco covering of the polychrome columns imitates marble on the upper section of the shafts.

Lighting from above in the home
Simple *atrium* in the Casa del Tramezzo di Legno (the house of the wooden screens), at Herculaneum. It is the plainest example of a structure with *impluvium* and *compluvium*, without recourse to columns to support the ceiling. In front of the entrance, a marble table stands before the pool of the *impluvium*.

RESTAVRATION
ECHELLE · 0,03 P·M·

POMPEI · MAISON · DV · CENTENAI

ECHELLE · 0,03 P·M·

POMPEI · MAISON · DV · CE

The splendor of patrician homes
Reconstruction by Jules-Léon Chifflot (1902) of the House of the Centenarian at Pompeii, in the form of a transversal section going from one *atrium* to the other, on the two levels of this luxurious house. The "restoration" of the paintings is based on contemporary archaeological discoveries, in particular on the frescoes in the house of the Vettii.

Bottom
Polychromy everywhere
Longitudinal section of the House of the Centenarian, according to Chifflot, with, from left to right, the vestibule, the main *atrium*, the *tablinum*, the large peristyle, followed by an *exedra* and a private garden.

NAIRE · RESTAVRATION

Dialogue with nature
The gardens of the house of
Loreius Tiburtinus, at Pompeii,
with their channels, ornamental
ponds, and arbors over the portico
that leads to the nymphaeum.

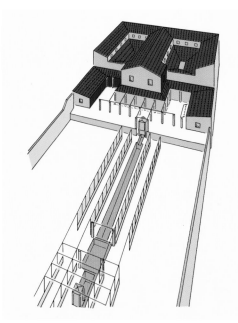

Dwelling in Pompeii
Perspectival view of the house of
Loreius Tibertinus. The arrange-
ment of the whole is symmetrical.
A hydraulic system dictates the
layout of the walled garden.

Wall painting in Pompeii
Detail from a painted design in the house of the Vettii. On the edge of a vast *frons scaenae* decor, an oblique viewpoint shows the airy buildings etched against the sky. A whole imaginary architectural world flourishes in the fourth style of Pompeian painting.

A sumptuous interior garden
The sumptuous peristyle surrounding the garden of the house of the Vettii at Pompeii, with its marble and bronze decorations. The stonework columns covered in stucco are made to look like marble.

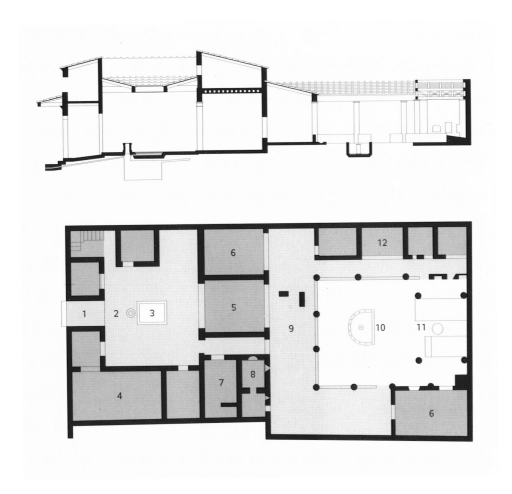

Layout of the home
Section and plan of the house of
Trebius Valens at Pompeii. The
longitudinal section goes from the
entrance to the *atrium*, crosses the
tablinium, and ends at the portico
of the peristyle, at the end of
which is a *triclinium*. The layout is
typical:
1. Vestibule
2. *Atrium*
3. *Impluvium*
4. *Triclinium*
5. *Tablinum*
6. Reception room
7. Kitchen
8. Bathroom
9. Porticoed peristyle
10. Fountain
11. Summer *triclinium*
12. *Exedra*

This play of space between the darkness of the enclosed rooms and the luminosity of the *atrium* and the interior garden became considerably more sophisticated in the large villas in the immediate environs of the city (Villa dei Misteri).
Here, in addition to the peristyle of the interior garden, the villa was surrounded
on its outer side by columned porticoes overlooking the landscape. The most
interesting room in this respect was the large reception room in the shape of an
exedra, whose semicircular bay opened up the view. In short, there existed a formula based on a succession of varied spaces, often placed on a single axis and
leading from the center of the house outwards towards the periphery: (1) the interior garden surrounded with porticoes; (2) the *atrium*; (3) the *tablinum*; and (4) the
exedra overlooking the countryside. This formula was peculiar to the opulent
patrician houses situated outside the town.

Page 109
Herculaneum
General view of the ruins of Herculaneum, whose buildings go
right down to the sea. In the distance, modern houses stand on an
accumulation of several meters of
lava that submerged the ancient
town in 79. In the foreground is
the colonnade that surrounded
the palestra, which extended to
the left.

Verandas and balconies

Timber-framed house on the *Cardo IV* at Herculaneum. It is a light construction, the stonework is consolidated with wooden structures (as a precaution against earthquakes). It projects over the street, with its balcony supported by brick columns (recreated). The name of this Casa a Gratticcio derives from its balustrade with cross-bars.

Page 111 top
First century wall painting
Mural painting showing Venus in a shell, in the peristyle of a house in Pompeii that bears her name. Reclining languidly on a couch in the form of a seashell, the goddess is surrounded by a veil that billows out in the breeze, in the form of a niche or a canopy, symbol of her divine status. This fresco, in the fourth Pompeian style, dates from A.D. 62–79.

Page 111 bottom
The enclosed garden, a haven of peace
The peristyle of the Casa di Venere on the eastern side of Pompeii is adorned with stonework columns with a polychrome stucco covering. In the background, the walls of the villa are entirely covered in paintings. This view gives an idea of the interpenetration of external and internal space of a Roman dwelling.

"Luxe, calme et volupté" of the baths
Heated room of the *tepidarium* in the forum baths (Terme del Foro) in Pompeii. Entirely covered in decorative stucco, the room is surrounded by niches supported by telamons. Bathers left their clothes here. This public bath dates from the first century B.C.

A lifestyle associated with water ritual
The *frigidarium* of the Terme del Foro at Pompeii is a small, domed room lit by an *oculus* in which a pool of icy water enabled bathers to cool off after the heat of the *laconicum* (steam bath).

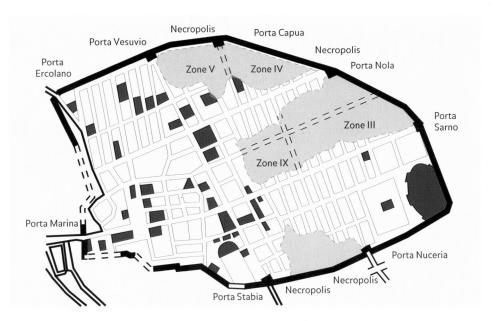

Plan of the walled city of Pompeii
The areas marked in gray have not yet been excavated by archaeologists.

View of a bedroom

Even the largest Pompeian homes had small bedrooms (*cubiculum*). Here in the Casa della Caccia antica (House of the Ancient Hunt) in Pompeii, the room is decorated with very spare paintings on a white background in the third and fourth style. Polychrome panels decorate the center of the composition. Some of them were removed before the modern excavations in order to satisfy the taste of eighteenth-century collectors.

Visual Art in the Home

In urban Pompeian houses, the lack of ground-floor openings to the outside meant that the house was entirely turned in on itself, forming an enclosed whole. The centripetal nature of this arrangement needed some form of decoration to mitigate the feeling of confinement. The inner garden surrounded by the colonnaded portico already provided an element of escapism. The Romans lavished great attention on careful planting and fountains, which helped to animate an artificial "landscape": evergreen shrubs (box, laurel, myrtle, etc.) alternated with flower beds. Nevertheless, the need for a less confined environment and a wider horizon soon made itself felt. Wall painting took up this role, and the great numbers uncovered at Pompeii, Herculaneum, and Stabia represent a dazzling discovery. This is perhaps the most captivating element of the cities of Vesuvius, allowing the observer to follow the evolution of representational art, domestic or palatial, over three centuries and giving a better understanding of the preoccupations of its citizens. The discovery of the everyday decor of Roman life completely transformed our understanding of architecture, since it enriched it with a particu-

Mosaic of Neptune and Amphytrite
This mosaic decorates the court-yard of a house in Herculaneum to which it gave its name (Casa del Mosaico di Nettuno e Anfitrite). The sumptuous scene, surmounted by a shell-shaped motif, over-looks the couch of an open-air *triclinium*.

Lavish atrium
In the house of Epidius Rufus at Pompeii, on the Via dell'Abbon-danza, the sixteen-columned *atrium* is classified as Corinthian – although its columns are Doric – in that it consists of a peristyle around the *impluvium*.

lar element, inherited from Hellenistic art and progressively adapted to Roman concerns. These concerns, which continued to stress the characteristics inherited from Alexandrian art and the subsequent artistic developments of the Diadochian courts of the Lagid, Attalid, and Seleucid monarchs, crystallized around two major poles: the enlargement of the pictorial horizon reflected the geographic expansion of Roman power that was enveloping the entire Mediterranean region, and an aspiration toward an ideal transcendental world that subsumed the individual into an eternal existence.

This double evolution can be seen in the variety of styles in the wallpaintings in Pompeian homes. These different varieties were classified as styles by August Mau more than a century ago, and since then, we have spoken of the "four styles" of Roman painting. In reality, this reference to style is more relevant to the content than to formal concerns. In addition, with the exception of the first style, the proposed chronological order Mau suggests is notional, since these so-called styles consistently coexist and blend with one another.

The first style, which lasted from approximately 200 to 80 B.C., was limited to simple mural polychromy, that imitated stone blocks of different colors, resorting to fake marble as well as illusionistic stucco. By then, wall space was divided into three superimposed horizontal zones, stylobate, main level, and upper frieze, an arrangement imitating the subdivision of load-bearing elements (columns or pilasters) according to the classical arrangement of base, column, and capital. The need for symmetry, strongly present in the ancient world, brought about vertical division: the central part of the wall space was flanked by two narrower panels. This division of the wall surface into three panels suited the demands of figurative painting, which generally adopted a symmetrical perspective, particularly for architectural compositions.

This is exemplified in the second style. It was based on spatial illusionism depicted within the confines of a constricted space, the wall acting as a window open onto the world outside, but it also depicted an image of a better world where man and god coexisted. In order to achieve this aim, it was necessary to create a pictorial language capable of transcending reality.

This pictorial art exploded the spatial confines of the room, while at the same time depicting scenes minutely observed from nature. The architectural setting conformed to the overall perspective. The perspective obeyed strict conventions that did not, however, always conform to a unified composition governed by one focal point. Nevertheless, the succession of planes, the distances glimpsed through open bays, and the sweep of colonnades all pointed to a clear awareness of spatial concerns.

In the center of the panels, the painter sometimes depicted mythological scenes ensconced in an idyllic landscape. Such a landscape symbolized an ideal garden that extended the garden of the peristyle, but by transposing it into the other world. It took on the character of a paradise (*paradeisos*) similar to those visualized in the Hellenistico-Parthian palaces. This preoccupation with Eden was contemporaneous with the monarchical ambitions of Sulla and the end of the Republican era. It expressed itself by a strictly organized pictorial representation of the desired mythical space.

The paradisical element became more pronounced in the third style, which flourished at the beginning of the Empire. It opened up an irrational world, aspiring more than ever to an eternal and superhuman reality. It was a general celebration of immortality couched in a dreamlike ambience. Thus a transcendental, sublime environment was created around the real garden in the center of the peristyle, much in the manner of a sacred grove adjoining the couches of the *triclinium*, used for family celebrations as well as ritual feasts.

Dining room of a villa

A covered *triclinium*, in the vast house of Julia Felix at Pompeii. Arranged in a U shape, the three marble couches of this winter dining room surround a central table.

In the Image of the Palace of the Gods

The godlike aspect was underlined in these paintings by the omnipresence of royal symbols: canopies and *tholos* were included in the center of a theatrical scene. The *frons scaenae*, or stage wall, was generally considered the typical habitat of gods and goddesses, a place where apparitions occurred and where the gods manifested themselves. Such a vision presupposes a conventional setting: multistoried columns, small *ciborium*-shaped constructions, and alternating projections and alcoves served to create the illusion of a celestial city. This luminous image of a structured, hierarchical paradise influenced many mural decorations in the Vesuvian cities.

August Mau defined a fourth style, although the definition is largely superfluous. The magic illusionism became more baroque and accentuated in Nero's time, followed by a classicism during Vespasian's reign, on the eve of the catastrophe. In technical terms, the sophistication of the artists reached its peak with these third and fourth styles. The delicate forms of the landscape created an atmosphere that shimmered with light, prefiguring the experiments of Turner and the impressionists.

In contrast to these idyllic scenes, the architectural compositions were very elaborate. Through art, the realization of these ideal, ethereal cities was possible, reflecting the more urgent spiritual aspirations of the beginning of Empire. Such a preponderance of architecture in Roman painting is significant; the world in which the Romans desired to live is reflected in these celestial palaces. If they resemble

Reconstruction of a wallpainting
During the excavations of Pompeii in the nineteenth century, painters and draftsmen made records – often completed and "restored" from other sources – that helped to visualize the original appearance of the painted decor of Roman houses. This example, with its center panel and the oblique perspective of its side panels, showing imaginary architectural composition, belongs to the fourth style. It shows a typical *frons scaenae*, with its tripartite composition.

An image of halcyon days
This record, by Niccolini in 1887, conforms to the triple subdivision in both horizontal and vertical terms of the painted decor of Pompeian villas. In the central section/medallion, the illustrator has depicted a scene showing Aphrodite fishing, inspired by a painting that adorns the house of Laocoon in the VIth district of the town (Regio VI).

Wallpainting in the *tablinum* of the Casa della Caccia antica
"The House of the Ancient Hunt" at Pompeii where the artist painted the surface of the lower register to resemble a polychrome marble covering and a hunting scene on a white background above it.

A love of bright colors
On either side of a central stucco molding, the colors used by the Romans in their homes achieve a remarkable degree of variety and luminosity. This is a detail from a decoration in the second style in the house of the Vettii at Pompeii.

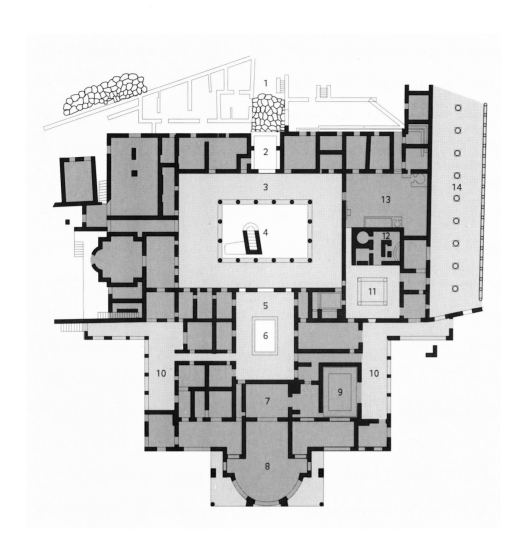

Villa dei Misteri at Pompeii

Plan of a large Roman dwelling at Pompeii: the Villa dei Misteri, built in the second century B.C. Around 60 B.C., ceremonial rooms were decorated with sumptuous second-style paintings.

 1. Entrance
 2. Vestibule
 3. Porticoed peristyle
 4. Garden and cistern
 5. *Atrium*
 6. *Impluvium*
 7. *Tablinum*
 8. Exedra-shaped reception room
 9. Room of the Dionysiac mysteries
10. Porticoes
11. Tetrastyle *atrium*
12. Baths
13. Kitchen overlooking courtyard
14. Double lateral portico

Pompeian wallpainting

Landscape with villa, pavilions, and pools, where figures are shown fishing and walking. This type of imaginary scene illustrates the ideal of Roman splendor. (Museo Nazionale, Naples)

Fresco in the palace of Empress Poppea
A fledgling pecking at some figs. A detail from a wall in the palace at Oplontis (Torre Annunziata) of the Empress Poppea, wife of Nero, dating from the beginning of the second half of the first century A.D.

Wallpainting in the Villa dei Misteri
Two details from the famous frescoes of the Villa dei Misteri at Pompei. Depicting an initiation to the mysteries of Dionysos, they date from 60 B.C. (second style).
Left: The look of fear on a woman's face at the apparition of the symbols of divinity.
Right: A naked dancer playing the castanets attends the flagellation scene of the initiate.

stage designs, it is because tragedies showed kings and gods of the mythical universe on the stage. Most of all, since the time of Philip II and the Hellenistic kings, the theater had become the focus of sacred processions. The statues of the gods with whom the rulers identified themselves were presented in the context of the court ritual, demonstrated in the case of temples built by Sulla at Praeneste and Tivoli.

Such were the decorations, in very bright colors, with vermilion red, black, blue, and yellow ochre dominating, with which well-to-do Romans liked to surround themselves. They transformed the house into a divine home, and its inhabitants into the elect of a Garden of Eden. In this pictorial art, the many symbolic allusions serve to reinforce their message. The Roman world, too often described as realist, even material, reveals here its dimension of intense religiosity, based on

The Amphitheater of Pompeii
Built in 80 B.C., the amphitheater of Pompeii (135 by 104 meters) is the oldest in the Roman world. Its exterior arcades and access stairways to the *cavea* buttress the seating area, which could hold 12 000 spectators.

an awareness of the destiny of the individual who expressed himself *hic et nunc* in his everyday surroundings, conceived in the image of a superior ideal.

It is true that Roman art would not have remained totally unknown if Vesuvius had not miraculously preserved hundreds of paintings. Indeed, remains discovered in Rome, in the house of Augustus, at the Farnesina, at Ostia, and in sanctuaries and tombs, all offer good painted examples. But the omnipresence of pictorial decoration in daily life would never have been suspected without the ruins uncovered at Pompeii, Herculaneum, and Stabia.

Most of all, it would not have been so clear that the Roman ideal resided in an eternal architectural and landscaped world of which the garden in the family's house, in the middle of its peristyle, was but a pale reflection, the *analogon* of an infinitely more wonderful Eden that haunted men's minds.

Page 121
A hall for Pompeian music lovers
Built into the hillside, the *cavea* of the small theater of Pompeii formed a hemicycle fitting into the slope, as its Greek predecessors did. This building is an "odeon," originally covered by a wooden roof, and could accommodate 800 to 900 spectators. Its construction dates from 80 B.C.

Pliny the Younger (62–114) describes his Villas

Every citizen's idea of Eden
In order to grasp the charm of Roman villas, one need only contemplate this Pompeian painting depicting a semicircular portico by the sea, with its piers and arbors. This work, from the Casa del Citaredo, was discovered during the excavations of 1859. (Museo Nazionale, Naples)

In his *Letters* (Book II, 17), Pliny describes, for the benefit of his correspondent Gallus, a visit to his villa of Laurentum, near Ostia, listing its various qualities:

"The house is large enough for my needs but not expensive to keep up. It opens into a hall, unpretentious but not without dignity, and then there are two colonnades, rounded like the letter D, which enclose a small but pleasant courtyard. This makes a splendid retreat in bad weather, being protected by windows and still more by the overhanging roof.

Opposite it, in the middle, is a cheerful inner hall, and then a dining room which really is rather fine: it extends out towards the shore, and whenever the sea is driven inland by the southwest wind it is lightly washed by the spray of the spent breakers. It has folding doors or windows as large as the doors all round, so that at the front and sides it seems to look out on to three seas, and at the back has a view through the inner hall, the courtyard with two colonnades, then the entrance hall to the woods and the mountains in the distance.

To the left of this and a little farther back from the sea is a large bedroom, and then another smaller one which lets in the morning sunshine through one window and holds the last rays of the evening sun with the other; from this window too is a view of the sea beneath, this time at a safe distance.

In the angle of this room and the dining-room is a corner which retains and intensifies the concentrated warmth of the sun, and this is the winter quarters and gymnasium of my household for no winds can be heard there except those which bring rain clouds, and the place can still be used after the weather has broken.

Round the corner is a room built round an apse to let in the sun as it moves round and shines in each window in turn, and with one wall fitted with shelves like a library to hold the books which I read and read again.

Next comes a bedroom-wing on the other side of a passage which has a floor raised and fitted with pipes to receive hot steam and circulate it at a regulated temperature. The remaining rooms on this side of the house are for the use of the slaves and freedmen, but most of them are quite presentable enough to receive guests."

In the rest of the letter, Pliny mentions yet more rooms built on the other side of the main core of the building. Then he describes the baths:

"Then comes the cold room (*frigidarium*), which is large and spacious and has two curved baths built out from opposite walls; these are quite large enough if you consider that the sea is so near. Next come the oiling-room, the furnace room, and the hot room (*hypocaustum*) for the bath, and then two rest-rooms, beautifully decorated in a simple style, leading to the heated swimming pool which is much admired and from which swimmers can see the sea.

Close by is the ball court which receives the full warmth of the setting sun. Here there is a second story, with two living rooms below and two above, as well as a dining room which commands the whole expanse of the sea and stretch of shore with all its lovely houses."

A typical Epicurean, Pliny continues to enumerate the pleasures offered by this villa of Laurentum, with its gardens and its walks lined with box, rosemary, vines, blackberry bushes, and fig trees. He mentions a vaulted cryptoporticus "nearly as large as a public building," the pleasures of a breezy terrace, and a pavilion, "truly my favorites, for I had them built myself," with a glazed veranda where one could recline "far from the murmuring of the sea."

Pliny and his Villas on Lake Como and in Tuscany

Pliny also described two other villas that he owned on Lake Como (*Letters* , Book IX, 7):

"The former has a wider view of the lake, the latter a closer one, as it is built to curve gradually round a single bay, following its line by a broad terrace; while the other stands on a high ridge dividing two bays, where a straight drive extends for some distance above the shore. One is untouched by the water and you can look down from its height to the fishermen below, while the waves break against the other and you can fish from it yourself, casting your line from your bedroom window and practically from your bed as if you were in a boat."

He owned yet another villa in Tuscany (Book V 6):

"My property is some distance from the sea, and is in fact at the very foot of the Apennines, which are considered the healthiest of mountains.

The countryside is very beautiful. Picture for yourself a vast amphitheater such as could only be a work of nature; the great spreading plain is ringed round with mountains, their summits crowned by ancient woods of tall trees, where there is a good deal of mixed hunting to be had.

Below them the vineyards spreading down every slope weave their uniform pattern far and wide, their lower limit bordered by a plantation of trees. Then come the meadows and cornfields.

My house is on the lower slopes of a hill but commands as good a view as if it were higher up. It faces mainly south, and so from midday onward in summer (a little earlier in winter) it seems to invite the sun into the colonnade. This is broad, and long in proportion, with several rooms opening out of it as well as the old-fashioned type of entrance hall. In front of the colonnade is a terrace laid out with box hedges clipped into different shapes, from which a bank slopes down, also with figures of animals cut out of box facing each other on either side. On the level below there is a bed of acanthus so soft one could say it looks like water. From the end of the colonnade projects a dining room: through its folding doors it looks on to the end of the terrace, the adjacent meadow, and the stretch of open country beyond, while from its windows ... on the other side can be seen the tree-tops in the enclosure of the adjoining riding ground." Pliny then described the living quarters. He mentioned a room surrounded by the branches of a plane tree, whose window frames are made of marble. "Inside is 'a fresco of birds perched on the branches of trees.' Here a painted image of a garden decorates the room with 'a small fountain with a bowl surrounded by tiny jets which together make a lovely murmuring sound.'"

Pliny's descriptions, sensitive as they are to the landscape and nature, albeit tamed, prove how attentive the Romans of Trajan's and Hadrian's time were to their surroundings. Pliny loved the country, but he was a town dweller who resorted to the most refined innovations. These descriptions give only a slight idea of the luxury of the imperial palaces.

Pliny used glazed windows in his villa, permitting enjoyment of the view. Central heating came from the steam of hypocausts. He swam in pools from which he could see the sea, the height of refinement. There was an abundance of fountains and pressurized water spouts murmuring aloud in the nymphaeum. Underground cryptoporticoes provided coolness in the height of summer. Behind the house, the sandy tracks of the hippodrome allowed him to ride on horseback. A ball court was available to players, and the gymnasium encouraged vigorous exercise. In short, everything was provided for an exceptional standard of living. And the country houses that Pliny owned, from the outskirts of Ostia to Lake Como, were endowed with every modern amenity.

Wallpainting in Herculaneum
A vividly painted sketch from Herculaneum showing a villa and its porticoes freely disposed in the landscape, with an aqueduct in the distance. (Museo Nazionale, Naples)

Trajan's Grand Plan
for the Heart of Rome

The Construction of the Forum
by Apollodorus

Page 125
Portrait of the Emperor Trajan
The great Emperor (98–117) in the
guise of victor, wearing a crown
of oak leaves and the breastplate
of the *imperator*.
(Museo Capitolino, Rome)

**Fresco representing Bacchus
holding the thyrsis**
This work, from the beginning of
the second century A.D. comes
from a Roman house discovered
under the baths of Caracalla. It
underlines the androgynous character of the Dionysiac divinity.
(Museo dell'Antiquario Palatino,
Rome)

Following Domitian's sudden death at the age of 44, victim of an assassination in
A.D. 96, the Senate, after a short interval, called upon one of its own, Nerva, to
take up the reins of Empire. Known for his wisdom and restraint, Nerva was
already elderly when he acceded to ultimate office. He was to occupy it for only
16 months, but in that time he restored order in the country and completed
Domitian's urban plan for the center of Rome, the Forum Transitorium.

Built on the models of the forums of Caesar and Augustus and situated
bet-ween Vespasian's Temple of Peace, inaugurated in 75, and the Temple of
Mars Ultor, this Forum Transitorium (so named on account of the narrowness of
the plot of land) allowed a glimpse of the Temple of Minerva through its colonnade. This Corinthian hexastyle temple has completely disappeared. The shame
brought about by Domitian's, *damnatio memoriae* meant that this scheme,
consecrated in A.D. 98 by the new septuagenarian emperor, was renamed the
Forum of Nerva.

By renaming this urban complex, the Romans showed that they truly wished,
at the dawn of the Antonine dynasty, to forget the excesses of the assassinated
predecessor. They aspired to a new age. The emperors of this "blessed period"
(*felicia tempora*), Trajan, Hadrian, Antoninus, and Marcus Aurelius, represent a
"golden century." Their reign created a period of stability and excellence. With
Hadrian's reign, a new era of peace began, comparable to the 40 years of Augustus's rule, marked by the famous *pax Augusti*.

Even before this auspicious period had begun, Trajan, who was nominated in
A.D. 97 as coparticipant to the principate, enlarged the frontiers of the *orbis
romanus* to their farthest point. As if in a supreme, last effort, the forces of Empire
pushed back the limits of territorial possessions on all fronts.

A "Spanish" Emperor

Trajan was born in A.D. 53 in Italica near Seville in the south of Spain, son of a
patrician family. His accession to power in A.D. 98 confirmed the importance that
the more distant provinces of the empire were assuming. Consequently, Spain was
to benefit from imperial favors, and the results were visible throughout the southern part of the country (Baetica), as well as at Mérida.

Trajan, a soldier by nature, conducted his principate like a true conqueror. Campaign followed campaign: in 101–102, then in 105–106, a merciless struggle
opposed him to the Dacians (Romania) and their king Decebalus; in 106 he conquered Petra and the kingdom of the Nabateans, which became the province of
Arabia; in 107, Dacia became a Roman province; from 114, he threw himself into a
long, arduous campaign against the Parthians in Mesopotamia and Armenia. Trajan died in 117 in the south of Anatolia on his way back from these battles that had
taken him all the way to the Persian Gulf. The empire now covered a vast area of
Europe and Asia. Having spread from the Mediterranean region, it stretched from
the Atlantic to Mesopotamia, from (Great) Britain to the Sahara, and from the
Crimea to Nubia. It had not only reached its greatest territorial dimension but also

Both a commemorative monument
– it recorded the war against the
Dacii – and a funerary one –
Hadrian placed the ashes of his
predecessor there –, Trajan's
Column constitutes the main sur-
vivor of the forum built by Apollodorus of Damascus. Isolated
today, the column once stood
behind the Basilica Ulpia,
between the Greek and Latin
libraries on the forecourt of the
temple of the deified Trajan.
At the summit, 40 meters above
the city, the gilt bronze statue of
the emperor contemplated his
creation.

possessed a strong sense of cohesion and cultural unity, due to the remarkable integration of the various provinces.

Trajan's political achievements earned him the title of *Optimus princeps*, the best of rulers. This appellation is based on an assumption that was in those days taken for granted. In the same way as in the Middle Ages the king was God's anointed one, so the righteous prince was elected the best among men by the gods. Such a choice by superior forces was to pave the way for the *imperator* to become the object of worship and to proceed to deification, ultimately to apotheosis.

Apollodorus, Imperial Architect

In the manner of an efficient supreme commander used to triumphing over all adversities, Trajan surrounded himself with brilliant and competent specialists.

Among these was one Apollodorus of Damascus, whose achievements were to be far-reaching. Between 102 and 105, this brilliant engineer constructed a huge bridge of wood over the Danube, indispensable for the movement of troops into Dacia. Its construction is depicted on the reliefs of Trajan's column.

Although of Asian origin, Apollodorus very probably learned his art in the imperial military schools. When Trajan decided to commemorate his reign by a grandiose project in the heart of Rome, he named Apollodorus chief architect, entrusting him with the responsibility of the enterprise. By this initiative, the emperor adopted an approach that would be common in the Renaissance: many artists had initially excelled as engineers in siegecraft, beginning with Francesco di Giorgio and Leonardo da Vinci. Similarly, in the sixteenth century, Suleiman the Magnificent entrusted the construction of his great mosques to Sinan, previously a member of the Janissary corps who in that role had built bridges, aqueducts, city walls, fortresses and war machines.

A Grandiose Project: The Forum of Trajan

The architectural work Apollodorus created is the Forum of Trajan, built from A.D. 107 to 112. The *imperator* intended to create a huge public space at the foot of the Quirinal hill to the northwest of the imperial forums, of Caesar, of Augustus, of Nerva, and of Vespasian, which would amount to the same surface area as all the earlier forums put together. It was an ostentatious project that well expressed the immensity of the empire and the glory of its master.

The first step in carrying out this gigantic project, which measured 300 by 190 meters, covering 5.5 hectares, was to expropriate populated areas. Then the engineers carried out a monumental program of terracing and leveling, which involved stabilizing the terrain and cutting into the southern slope of the Quirinal.

Trajan was able to realize this ambitious program thanks to the riches pillaged from the Dacians. The vision he adopted, and that Apollodorus translated into reality, aimed to restore to the forum its original function: a public space at the disposition of the Roman people. Such were the general aims of the scheme, developed on an east-west axis.

Only a few scattered traces remain of this immense marble creation, which constituted the center of the capital's civic life until the year 800. An earthquake seriously damaged it in 801, and the ruins were plundered by lime burners. But pre-

Left

Trajan commemorates his victory
A 200 meter frieze spirals around Trajan's column, forming an extraordinary narrative illustrating the exploits of the Dacian wars (A.D. 101–107). The monument, built entirely of Carrara marble, whose reliefs were once painted, was inaugurated in A.D. 112.

Right

A war chronicle extolling peace
Detail of the shallow relief of Trajan's column in Rome. Here we see the construction of a fortification by legionnaires. The diversity of the themes treated the whole length of this "cartoon strip" chronicle provides a precious source of information on ancient techniques.

cious details describing it survive in the *forma urbis severiana*, a plan of ancient Rome traced in marble between 205 and 208 in the time of Septimius Severus, which was deposited in the annex of Vespasian's Temple of Peace, where its many fragments were later unearthed.

Moreover, the excavations published in 1897 and 1933, Italo Gismondi's restoration dating from 1941, and new investigations undertaken since 1972 by the American archaeologist James E. Packer have enriched our knowledge of the Forum of Trajan, giving a precise picture of its general appearance and the detail of its ornamentation. It is now possible to make a well-informed reconstruction of the scheme, that makes the admirable achievements of Apollodorus even more evident.

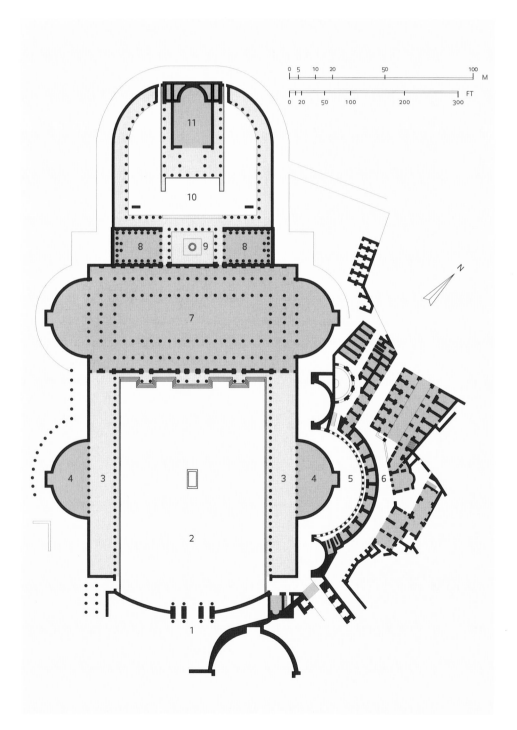

Plan of the Forum of Trajan
The Forum of Trajan was built in Rome between A.D. 107 and 112 by the architect Apollodorus of Damascus:
1. Triumphal entrance arch
2. Square surrounded by porticoes
3. Marble-columned porticoes
4. *Exedras*
5. Markets of Trajan
6. Via Biberatica
7. Basilica Ulpia with its two *exedras*
8. Greek and Latin libraries
9. Trajan's column
10. Courtyard of the Temple of Trajan surrounded by porticoes
11. Temple of the deified Trajan, built by Hadrian.

Graphic reconstruction of the Forum of Trajan in Rome
This reconstruction is based on the results of research by the archaeologist James E. Packer and his school. The transversal Basilica Ulpia blocks off the perspective of the square. In the center, an equestrian statue of the emperor. Bigas and one quadriga in bronze stood on the top of the entrance portico of the basilica.

The Triumph of Space

The monumental entrance, situated on the western side of the Forum of Augustus, consisted of a facade whose rounded form was reminiscent of the entrance to a circus: three juxtaposed triumphal arches forming a circular arc. In order to stress the analogy with the arena of a hippodrome, they were surmounted by a gilt bronze quadriga driven by the emperor. Once through the triumphal gates, the visitor advanced into a huge paved square (116 by 95 meters), surrounded by porticoes of solid white marble columns. The open area with the equestrian statue of Trajan in its center was flanked right and left behind the colonnades by two semicircular *exedras*. To the north, slightly recessed, stood the markets of Trajan, the only buildings of this vast enterprise that survive today. Over six stories high, they stand against the Quirinal hill, forming the commercial quarter. The whole width at the end of the square of the forum was taken up by a large building transversally placed, with three entrances side by side, surmounted by a quadriga flanked by two bigas. This was the Basilica Ulpia (after the emperor's family name: Marcus Ulpius Trajanus). This sumptuous building consisting of five naves with an apse at either end in the role of *exedras*, formed a transversal entity no less than 165 meters long, in effect, the largest basilica ever built in the empire: Its inside area reached 104 by 52 meters. Its pillars and white marble columns, its upper attic galleries, its wooden coffered roof, its bronze tiles mentioned by Pausanius: everything celebrated grandeur and supreme elegance in this sumptuous hall. Behind the Basilica Ulpia was a small, porticoed square surrounding Trajan's column, a monument both curious and colossal. Almost 40 meters high, this gigantic column, crowned by a huge gilt bronze statue of Trajan wearing his breastplate, presented the whole illustrated account of the war against the Dacians, sculpted in a helicoidal strip that, unraveled, would measure approximately 200 meters in length.

A place to converse, plead,
and harangue in the shade of the
porticoes

The most recently discovered
remains of the Forum of Trajan en-
able one to reconstruct the appearance of the porticoes at the edge
of the square. Square pillars (on
the right) corresponded to the
Corinthian colonnade in white
marble (to the left), marking the
limit of the *exedras*. The vaulted
ceiling itself was built in light
stonework covered in polychrome
stucco.

Two libraries, one Greek, the other Latin, stood on either side of this small
courtyard, reflecting a similar arrangement at the Temple of Peace in the Forum of
Vespasian. These two halls, both 30 meters long, with two stories of colonnades
on the inside, were apparently covered by intersecting groined vaults, according
to the usual formula adopted for basilical halls and Roman baths.

Finally, behind this complex, a vast semicircular esplanade surrounded by porticoes was the site where, on the death of the emperor, a temple dedicated to the
deified Trajan (*divus Trajanus*) was built by Hadrian, his adopted son, heir, and successor. It consisted of an octostyle sanctuary placed on the alignment formed by
the quadriga of the triumphal entrance, the equestrian statue in the middle of the
square, the central axis of the Basilica Ulpia, and, finally, Trajan's Column.

Page 133
The libraries of Trajan's Forum
The team led by James E. Packer
has reconstructed the internal
space of the two libraries of the
Forum of Trajan in Rome. The
buildings with two-story Corinthian porticoes were covered by
cross vaults. In order to provide
lighting, transversal projections
were equipped with windows.
The load-bearing structure consisted of a two-shell formula that
conformed to the functional needs
of storage (deep alcoves) while
providing great stability.

The "supermarket" of the Roman capital
Still almost intact, this vast covered hall forms the commercial center of the upper level of the markets of Trajan. It operates on two stories. The concrete vault is made up of a series of lateral projections opening on to trading galleries, with their shops on the second story.

The Rebirth of the Forum

A striking feature of the Forum of Trajan is the extent to which the religious character of the complex was eclipsed. The rectangular Basilica Ulpia, at the end of the square, obscured and relegated, quite literally, the Temple of Trajan to the background. The latter is in fact the product of a second wave of building undertaken after the death of the emperor. This is no minor detail; it signals a revolution.

The forums of Caesar, Augustus, Vespasian, and Nerva all had the facade of a temple as focal point. In Trajan's forum, the decision to replace the religious monument with a civic building represented a fundamental change in emphasis. By replacing a religious area with a public square, Trajan demonstrated a change of attitude that was rich in significance. A place dedicated to civic activity was restored to the people of Rome, and the ambivalent relationship between sanctuary and basilica, represented by the temple of Mars Ultor, flanked by its two exedral basilicas, was brought to an end. Indeed a project to dedicate a temple to the deified emperor in the Forum of Trajan probably existed from the outset. But its intended position, hidden behind the Basilica Ulpia and the memorial column, deeply changed its significance. Thereafter, the sanctuary no longer dominated the scheme, even if it still represented the ultimate point in it.

General view of the semicircular *exedra* that forms the markets of Trajan in Rome.

This utilitarian complex, 60 meters in diameter, is built in brick with a covering of concrete. On the ground floor, halls intended for commercial use open up their large bays with windows above them on the first floor, behind which a passage gives access to the shops.

In reality, the focal point of the Forum of Trajan had once again become the square itself, the *agora* surrounded by porticoes, like Greek *stoas*. Here was a forum in the proper sense of the word, rather than a thoroughfare lined with porticoes leading to the podium steps of a temple whose presence polarized the space. In this area of almost square proportions, grand celebrations, official ceremonies, and receptions for ambassadors and allied sovereigns could take place.

The vast porticoes of the Basilica Ulpia were dedicated to judicial and political activities. It was the tribunal, in the full sense of the word, such as it was associated with the power of the prince dictating the law and decreeing its rules. In its halls, the *jus romanus* was proclaimed, major trials were held, and advocates, senators, and lawyers discussed the *res publica*.

In the two exedras stood colossal statues representing members of Trajan's family, the *gens Ulpia*. The emperor himself was represented in his various manifestations in the form of gigantic statues.

Behind the Basilica Ulpia, the two libraries formed the cultural complex of the *Forum Trajani*. They gathered together the written legacy of Graeco-Latin authors, the heritage, whether historic, literary, or scientific, of the past. It was the repository of a civilization.

The monument they flanked, Trajan's column, was the chronicle of Trajan. His feats of arms against the Dacians were exalted there. Was it a paean to war? On the contrary, it would seem that it constituted one of the first depictions of the horrors of war. The account shown on these shallow reliefs, unraveling like a *volumen*, does not shrink from showing the cruelty of battle, the pitiful state of the defeated, and the misery of the Dacians condemned to exile. It was perhaps an indicator of the desire for peace that Trajan's successors from Hadrian to Marcus Aurelius would seize on. Another memorial was the funerary monument forming the base of Trajan's Column, which housed the golden urn containing the ashes of the princeps brought back from Cilicia by Hadrian.

Finally, on the sanctuary's pediment, supported by shafts of granite 2 meters in diameter and almost 20 meters high, an image of the hero in his immortal incarnation was depicted. Inside the temple, the sovereign-god, the *divus Trajanus*, sat enthroned, like Jupiter, in the form of a colossal sculpture occupying the *cella*.

Such was the grandiose Apollodorian creation that governed the public life of Rome during several centuries and to which Trajan's successors made little alteration. It represents the synthesis of political, judicial, and religious life of the second century.

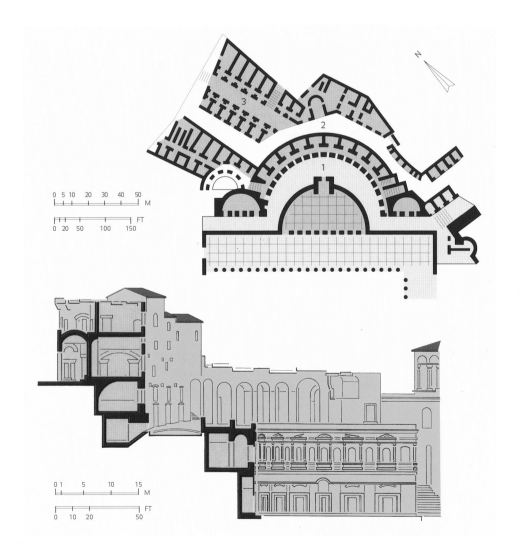

The markets of Trajan

Top

Plan of the semicircle of buildings built into the slope of the Quirinal hill.

1. Level of the *exedra* of the forum
2. Level of the Via Biberatica
3. Cross-vaulted commercial center.

Bottom

Schematic section of the markets of Trajan, with the buttressing systems built into the hill.

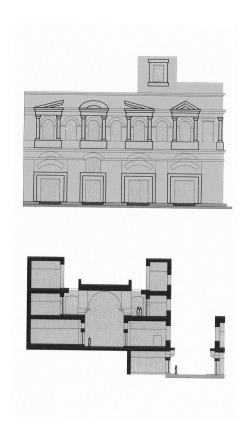

Utilitarian architecture
Top
Elevation of the semicircular facade of the markets of Trajan animated by relieving arches and pediments.
Bottom
Section of the upper level of the markets of Trajan, with the shopping gallery and, set below, the Via Biberatica.

Right
Brick and Marble
Detail of a bay on the lower level of the markets of Trajan. In the red-brick building, the white marble frame of the openings is surmounted by large semicircular relieving arches.

The Markets of Trajan

The economic and commercial aspect of Trajan's program was concentrated to the north of the *Forum Trajani*, behind the *exedra* at the edge of the imperial square. Built into the slope of the Quirinal hill in the shape of a six-story circular arc in the fashion of a *cavea*, the complex of the markets of Trajan fulfilled an essential role in a capital numbering approximately one million inhabitants.

In contrast to the official, ostentatious character of the white marble forum, the utilitarian character of the markets of Trajan was underlined by the use of brick for all the structures of their vast construction. Only the door frames stood out from the redness of the walls. The overall quality of the brick facing was remarkably good and demonstrated a high degree of attention to detail.

The ground floor and the first story stand in a vast semicircular sweep of 60 meters in diameter, punctuated with semicircular arched bays with alternately triangular and semicircular pediments. A third level stood recessed a little from the first two. (Nothing remains today of this third level.) Its shops overlooked the via Biberactica, which ran through the complex. On the other side of this street a rectilinear covered market survives, arranged on two stories forming the fourth and fifth levels of the overall structure. This large hall was covered by concrete cross-vaulting. Windows above the lateral gallery-like corridors provided ventilation and supplied indirect light.

Various spheres of activity were scattered in this large complex, housing the state warehouses, the administrative services supervising trade and fixing prices *(institutio alimentaria)*, the offices related to the *annona* (distribution of wheat), as well as the revenue offices that taxed economic activity and financed the treasury.

The Forum of Trajan represents a global, synthetic whole, where the sovereign had a succession of roles: administrator of the empire, supervising trade and commerce; victor of the farthest frontiers of the territory; legislator guaranteeing temporal law; Pontifex Maximus ordering the divine law; and deified ruler who attained apotheosis.

The Development of the Port of Ostia

In addition to the Forum of Trajan, various other projects were attributed to Apollodorus, among them an odeon (a small, covered theater), a circus, and a gymnasium. He is also sometimes thought to be the author of the vast hexagonal harbor called Portus. This artificial pool built opposite Ostia on the right bank at the Tiber's mouth was designed to encourage the development of the town. Ostia, the large port that fed the capital, experienced a vigorous urban expansion in the second century A.D.

It started out as a simple army fort established to prevent enemy ships sailing up the Tiber to Rome. Situated on a strip of land that projected toward the sea on the left bank of the river, this primitive fort, founded in 349 B.C., occupied only 2 hectares. Once the town began to grow, it adopted a gridlike pattern for its streets, becoming the earliest example of Roman town planning with *cardo* and *decumanus* departing at right angles from the capitol overlooking the forum.

During the second century B.C., Ostia grew laterally. The whole was now oriented north-south, and the straight portion of the *decumanus maximus*, 1500 meters long, followed the original course of the Tiber. In Sulla's time, toward 80 B.C., the Republican town built its city walls on a broadly rectangular plan.

The various districts of the town developed regularly to the east. It was along this axis that the large public buildings went up: the Augustan theater; the temple of Rome and Augustus; the capitol, rebuilt in Hadrian's time and dedicated to Jupiter; Juno, and Minerva, the public baths, and so forth. The first commercial harbor, intended to supply Rome and allowing the transfer of goods from ships too large to sail up the river, was built between 41 and 54 during the reign of Claudius.

The better-protected hexagonal port of Portus, built in Trajan's time, was linked to the sea by a narrow channel. A canal connected it to the river. Each side of the hexagon of the harbor pool was 370 meters long. A palace was built on the edge of it, and its installations, quays, docks, shops, and warehouses, formed the town of Portus, a potential rival to Ostia. But the two ports complemented each other, and Ostia gained from this presence.

Like Pompeii and the other Vesuvian towns, the preservation of Ostia was the result of an ecological disaster. Severe flooding by the river caused the abandonment of the site well before the medieval period. Mud and silt invaded the streets, homes, monuments, and technical installations. These floods and the changing course of the Tiber fostered the appearance of malaria, making the area uninhabitable and driving out the last inhabitants.

The significance of Ostia lies mainly in its dwellings – its shops and its warehouses – permitting a study of the *insulae* system, complementing the urban arrangement described at Pompeii and Herculaneum. The large blocks of apartments built at Ostia by the maritime and river companies to house their many

Mosaic floors in Ostia
Two details from the somewhat unpolished style of the black and white mosaics decorating the floors of Ostian homes: a dolphin, considered the protecting animal of mariners, and a winged river divinity.

Capitol of Ostia

The lofty structure of the capitol of Ostia, at the north of the forum of the town, consists of a sanctuary of brick originally faced in marble at the top of a large, central stairway. Consecrated to the capitoline triad, this hexastyle temple, built during the reign of Hadrian, was surrounded by a portico, traces of which survive today.

A man-made port

Schematic plan of the hexagonal port, whose sides measure 370 meters long, built – probably by Apollodorus – to the north of the mouth of the Tiber opposite Ostia. This construction, named Portus, was inaugurated in 113. It included a palace, a theater, and a thermal establishment that complemented the installations of Ostia. A lighthouse indicated its position to seafaring navigators.

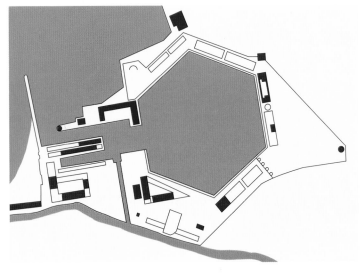

The Horrea Epagathiana at Ostia
General view of the *insula* that makes up the Horrea Epagathiana at Ostia, dating from Hadrian's time. This complex, with its imposing pedimented entrance leading to an interior courtyard, had two stories. It was the headquarters of an import-export business, with both shops and administrative offices.

Page 141
International trading house
Detail of the brick ornamentation of this commercial building belonging to a rich Graeco-oriental merchant. A skilful use of brick components allowed the vigorous expression of decoration, which would originally have been treated in stone.

Unembellished architecture
Elevation of the building that gives its name to the Via dei Balconi in Ostia. Occuping an *insula*, the building, consisting of two stories of living accommodation over the ground floor of shops largely open on to the street, is entirely built of brick. The overhanging arcades that support the balcony running around the building underline the two types of occupation of the building by separating them. This type of *insula* is characteristic of the period spanned by Trajan and Hadrian.

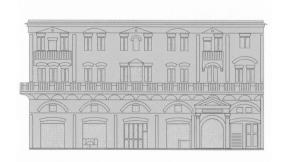

employees were made up of separate units on each floor. Their arrangement had little relation to the formula of the *atrium* and the interior garden of the Vesuvian villas but bears a marked resemblance to modern models. The urban plan of Ostia consists of large, multi-story *insulae* on a square or rectangular plan. Each block was built around an interior courtyard. Apartments consisting of three to eight rooms existed in the blocks.

The largest private buildings of the town belonged to maritime and river navigation companies, or to guilds and corporations of traders and financiers. These were buildings of the *horreum* type. For example, the Horrea Epagathiana of Ostia, belonging to a rich merchant, were three-story blocks where the ground floor was surmounted by a narrow balcony supported by corbelled arcades. The ground floor was reserved for shops and storage, broadly open to the street. The upper floors, with their typical double windows, consisted of administrative offices and private dwellings.

The significance of this brick-built utilitarian architecture, like the markets of Trajan, lies in the ornamental nature expressed by the builders in the simple rythmical arrangement of the units forming the *opus testaceum*, the visible brick facing. The masons not only built supporting arches, borders, cornices, and pediments with great virtuosity in brick, but also the embedded columns and the Tuscan capitals of the decoration, showing that they had become conscious of the importance of a material that until then had been neglected or even concealed by other surface materials.

Every port attracts visiting seamen and trips ashore. This is why Ostia consisted not only of leisure buildings (public baths and theater) but also a large number of bars and taverns, the *thermopolia* already discovered at Pompeii, that lined the streets and offered drinks, snacks, and hot food to passersby. At least 38 have been discovered in the town, a sign that trade was prosperous and that the harbor's commerce, intended to supply the capital, was healthy.

Page 143 top
Theater in Mérida
The handsome stage wall *(frons scaenae)* of Mérida's theater (Spain), whose *cavea* dates from the period of Augustus (A.D. 18), is the result of improvements carried out during Hadrian's reign, in the second century. With its projecting and recessed features and its canopies with arched pediments, this remarkably restored building illustrates the emblematic role of Roman ceremonial buildings.

The meeting place of the shipfitter
On a floor of black and white mosaic, the *thermopolium* of the Street of Diana at Ostia, with a bar standing in front of an elegant room of a restaurant decorated with paintings. The technique of a straight lintel of brick, under a large supporting arch, is typical of Roman architecture of the second century A.D.

Rich ornamentation
Detail of a Corinthian capital of the theater at Mérida. The rich ornamentation demonstrates that Spain benefited substantially from the attentions of imperial power, due to the fact that it was the homeland of several emperors of the Antonine dynasty.

The Golden Age of Roman Spain

During the rule of the "Spanish" emperors, it was normal that Roman Spain should experience significant progress. The close relations existing between Italy and Spain dated back to the Punic Wars. The dynamic presence of the Carthaginians in the Iberian peninsula constituted a threat to Rome. In 219 B.C., Hannibal was accused, with the capture of Sagonte, of having overstepped the limits that a treaty between the Romans and Carthaginians had fixed. It resulted in a bitter dispute that led to the Second Punic War.

After Hannibal almost won this war on Italian soil, he was beaten by Scipio in North Africa at the battle of Zama, near Carthage, in 202 B.C. Rome exploited the situation and annexed Spain but was confronted by the dogged resistance of the Celtiberian tribe that rose up on three separate occasions in 181, 154, and 144 B.C. The tragic end of the siege of the fortified town Numance, which had resisted Scipio Emilius for eight years, marked the end of the Spanish spirit of independence.

The riches of the Iberian peninsula were of great importance for Rome, in particular the silver mines in the northeast, as well as its rich agricultural and industrial resources. On the politico-cultural level, the Hispanic legacy is noteworthy: five Roman emperors were natives of Spain, and authors such as Seneca, Martial, Quintilian, Lucan, and Oroses are the glory of Latin literature.

The country was never really fully romanized until Augustus's reign, with the foundation of the colony of Augusta Emerita (Mérida), in 25 B.C., where the urban program typical of Roman cities came into play: temples, public baths, theater, and so forth. The theater of Mérida, one of the best examples known in the West,

Aqueduct of Segovia

Built during Trajan's reign, the aqueduct of Segovia measures more than 800 meters long. Its two levels of arcades built of large, dry blocks of granite dominate the valley by around 30 meters. Its 128 arches still carry the water conduit that supplies the upper town. It is one of the most remarkable achievements of Roman utilitarian architecture. The vibrations caused by vehicles now threaten this eighteen-century-old structure.

Baths of Alanga
Not far from Mérida, the baths of Alanga, with their two domed halls, 11 meters in diameter, lit by *oculi*, are still in use – testimony to the enduring nature of Roman creations.

was built during Augustus's reign, then enriched by a superb stage wall in the second century, during the reigns of Trajan and Hadrian. With its two levels of columns, enhanced by canopies and "baroque" recesses and projections, it is the product of a remarkable archaeological restoration, which gives an excellent idea of the *frons scaenae*, to which Karl Schefold attributes a dimension connected with the "supraterrestrial sphere," in much the same way as the Pompeian paintings.

Farther north, the town of Segovia possesses an aqueduct that Bernard Andreae considers the largest and most splendid of the whole of the Roman Empire. Built under Trajan, it dates from the first quarter of the second century A.D. and is 813 meters long by 30 meters high. Its 128 arches are built in large blocks of granite, assembled entirely without mortar.

The luxurious villa of Conimbriga and the temple of Evora in the province of Lusitania should not be omitted from this account, witnesses as they are to the penetration of Roman civilization right to the Atlantic coast.

These examples illustrate the importance of the westernmost province in the group of romanized regions and underline the quality of the ruins that survive there.

Page 147
Temple of Diana at Evora
At Evora in Portugal, the Corinthian hexastyle temple known as the Temple of Diana is an example of the expansion of Roman art in the second century A.D. The high podium, where the temple's fluted columns stand, has been stripped of its marble covering.

HADRIAN'S GENIUS

Hadrian, Architect and Emperor

Trajan's successor, Hadrian, was a native of southern Spain, like his adoptive father. He was born in A.D. 76 in Italica. After finishing his education in Rome, he entered the army at age 19, fought in Thrace and Germany, married Trajan's niece, and commanded a legion in Dacia at the side of his protector. Named consul in 108, he was charged with writing the speeches of the prince. From 113 to 117, he took part in the Mesopotamian campaign. On Trajan's death in Cilicia, Hadrian acceded to power at the age of 41.

The political philosophy of his reign (117–138) was one of total peace. He did not hesitate to abandon regions that were precarious, such as Mesopotamia and Armenia, choosing to concentrate on the defense of the *limes*. He constructed fortified lines in the places where danger threatened, in particular, building a huge wall in Scotland crossing the country from the Solway Firth to the Tyne estuary.

The only cloud on this peaceful horizon was the Jewish revolt in Palestine, which would not be overcome until A.D. 135. The empire was so peaceful that the emperor was able to absent himself from Rome for long periods, carrying out tours of inspection in faraway provinces. Hadrian traveled in this way from 121 to 126 and then from 129 to 134, taking with him the principal functionaries responsible for the smooth working of the *res public*. Moreover, he was also able to indulge his passion: architecture. Everywhere he went, he built temples, theaters, libraries, and stadia, and undertook major town planning schemes in many cities, in the western and eastern part of the Roman Empire alike.

A dedicated "philhellene," he venerated Greek culture, spending long periods in Athens. He spent some time there in 112 and 122, returning to spend the winters of 128–129, 131–132 and 132–133. During one visit, he was initiated into the mysteries at the sanctuary of Eleusis.

A Transitional Work: The Temple of Venus and Rome

Despite his veneration for Hellenic art, Hadrian's architectural creations were unmistakably Roman in character. Not content just to commission buildings, the emperor himself set down the main principles and modalities, and he personally was the creator of a series of masterpieces. Some have disappeared, but others are intact, demonstrating the genius of his designs. However, such a personality could not express itself without conflicting with other sensibilities, notably with the master builder, Apollodorus. It appears that Hadrian allowed him to finish the Forum of Trajan with the construction of the temple dedicated to the deified emperor, but their personalities soon clashed, and, according to some authors, the crisis culminated with Apollodorus being condemned to death.

The Temple of Venus and Rome, built near the Colosseum, numbers among the great constructions of Hadrian's reign. Although building work began in 121, the gigantic sanctuary was not dedicated until 137. The temple, a classic peripteral construction in a *temenos* 165 by 103 meters (1.7 hectares) surrounded by a portico, was a decastyle that contained two apses placed back to back. The resulting

The "Great Wall" of the western world
The emperor had the legions of (Great) Britain build Hadrian's Wall in Scotland. The defensive construction, intended to keep out the barbarian hordes of the north, is 117 kilometers long. Built between 122 and 124, it is 5 to 6 meters high and 2 to 3 meters wide.

A marvel of Roman technology
The dome of the thermal building known as the Temple of Diana at Baiae, near Naples, shows the virtuosity of the builders of the second century. This huge, flattened dome, which covers an area 29 meters in diameter (100 Roman feet), is extraordinarily thin in relation to its span.

double *cella* was 87 meters (300 feet) by 29 meters (100 feet). The size of its peristyle (108 by 54 meters) covered an area three times more vast than the Parthenon (approximately 70 by 30 meters). In broad terms of design, the Temple of Venus and Rome remains quite traditional. It might have been the last building on which Apollodorus was to collaborate. This could explain why it took 17 years to complete. The two apses that survive today in the center of the *temenos* are a restoration carried out around A.D. 300, during the rule of Maxentius.

The Building of the Pantheon

With the Pantheon, Hadrian gave full rein to his prodigious architectural genius. It was built in the Campus Martius on the site of the sanctuary that Agrippa had intended as a dynastic temple but which had been made into a pantheon at the behest of Augustus. Hadrian's building was not a simple "restoration job," as the inscription in bronze letters decorating the frieze, beneath the majestic pediment of the portico, would imply. Indeed the words read: "Made by Agrippa during his third consulate." If Hadrian had wanted the paternity of his monument attributed to the founder of the first pantheon, it was probably not through a sense of humility but to confirm that he was creating, as Agrippa had wanted, a new dynastic temple.

The Pantheon in Rome
Masterpiece of Emperor Hadrian in his role of builder, the Pantheon in Rome was started in 121 A.D. Its octostyle facade comprising 16 monolithic shafts of granite supports a classical pediment where the emperor restored the inscription of the first Pantheon built by Agrippa for Augustus. This portico hides the huge, blind rotunda whose external diameter reaches 58 meters (200 feet).

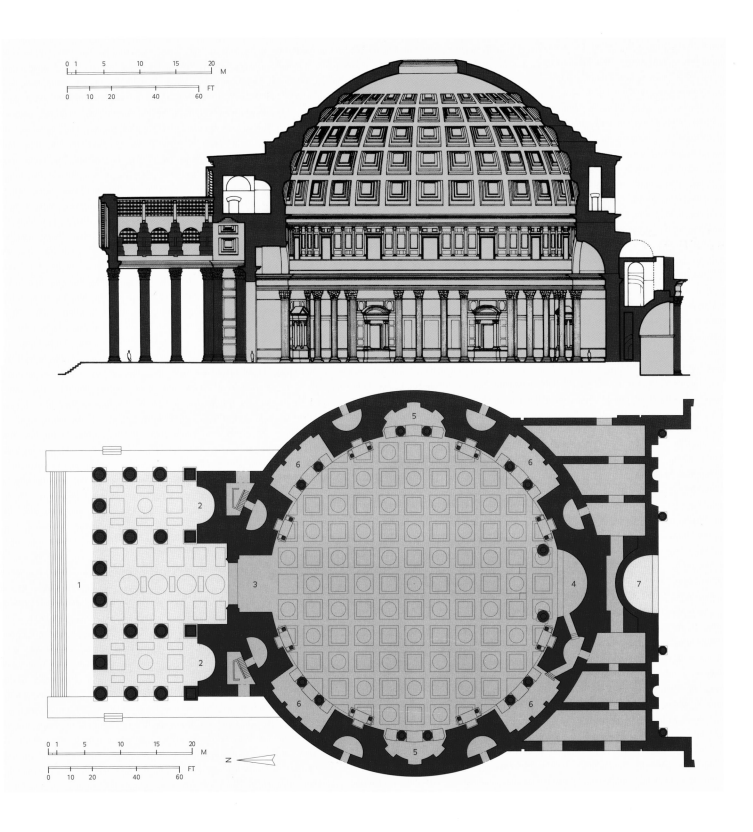

Architectural masterpiece

Top

Longitudinal section of the Pantheon, showing the vast interior space 44 meters (150 feet) in diameter covered by the flattened hemispherical dome of five levels comprising 28 coffers. The cylindrical base, divided into two levels, is equal to the height of the dome. The summit of the dome is 44 meters high at the *oculus*, which is 9 meters in diameter and constitutes the sole light source of the building.

Bottom

Plan of Hadrian's Pantheon
1. Entrance portico
2. Niches containing statues of Agrippa and Augustus
3. Entrance vestibule
4. Main apse situated on the longitudinal axis
5. Secondary apses in the form of semicircular *exedras*
6. Apses in the form of "rectangular" *exedras* on the diagonal axes
7. Apse of the basilica of Neptune

A vault in the image of the universe
Skyward view of the dome of the Pantheon in Rome. Around the large *oculus*, which, in the manner of the sun, lights the whole, the five levels of coffers represent the course of the five planets known to the Romans. The building reflects the geocentric system with its homocentric spheres that are codified in Ptolemy's cosmology.

An octostyle porch stands in front of the Pantheon's huge blind rotonda with a single light source from the central *oculus* at the top of the dome. Related to the contemporaneous dome of the thermal baths at Baiae (100 feet, or 29 meters in diameter) known as the Temple of Diana, the Pantheon is a sanctuary with all the characteristics of a thermal building. The cylindrical walls of the huge hall support a colossal dome, 44 meters in diameter on the inside. The span of this dome would never be surpassed during the Roman era. This unique achievement is all the more remarkable in that it has survived almost two millennia virtually without modification, for the building was transformed into a church in 609 on the order of the Byzantine emperor Phocas.

The proportions of the work were truly exceptional. If one includes the courtyard of porticoes (of which no trace remains) that stood in front of it, evoking the forums of Caesar and Augustus, the whole complex probably measured 200 meters in length. The rectangular entrance portico alone measured 400 by 200 feet. The proportions of the rotunda itself, built on an octagonal plan, are as follows: its external diameter is also 200 feet (58 meters) across; the internal circular space measures 150 feet in diameter to 150 feet in height (44 meters approximately) from the floor to the *oculus*, the latter 30 feet (9 meters) in diameter.

A study of the ground plan and the elevation of the rotunda is revealing. Behind the large porch that leads to the central entrance, flanked by two vast niches for statues, the circular hall contains seven apses – four of them rectangular and three of them semicircular (one of which is the main apse situated opposite the entrance). A pair of columns stands in front of each of these, as in the case of exedras. Eight small projecting structures with small columns and pediments stand between these apses.

Page 156
Tabernacles for divinities
Detail of the design and the polychrome marble veneer that form the internal decoration of the Pantheon. The building is particularly well preserved because it was transformed into a church in 609 A.D. Even the original statue niches still exist (where saints have replaced the ancient gods). According to Dion Cassius, images of Mars and Venus stood there alongside the deified Caesar, as well as other astral figures.

The walls of the hall are cylindrical. A cornice projects out midway up (75 feet or 22 meters). The height of the enormous hemispherical dome above reaches 22 meters. The dome has five concentric rows of trapezoidal coffers, each consisting of 28 coffers.

Before the invention of reinforced concrete, the realization of such an immense internal space, 1520 square meters without any intermediate supports and 46,000 cubic meters in all, required the mobilization of all the resources available to Roman technology. In that unified, homogeneous hall without apparent load-bearing elements, the whole thrust of the massive stonework dome relies on the cylindrical structure that forms the circle of retention. Despite appearances, this 6-meter-thick wall is not a solid mass. The cylindrical surround supporting the cupola consists, very ingeniously, of two separate thicknesses between which there are inaccessible, blind cavities. This two-layer arrangement, which achieves the optimum resistance for the smaller area, explains the stability of the Pantheon's walls.

Page 157
A spherical universe
The space of the Pantheon, inscribed within a spherical scheme, conveys an impression of indescribable grandeur that visitors cannot fail to sense. The originality of the design and the scale of the realization of this hall founded on an entirely closed shell, with the exception of the luminous *oculus*, has assumed since antiquity the status of a masterpiece displaying unmatched technological prowess.

In addition to these hidden cavities, which strengthen the base of the structure, the technological gamble was also carried off by using increasingly light materials towards the top of the dome. The horizontal layers over a core of travertine and tufa stonework were constructed first in brick, then in brick mixed with pumice. Finally, the circular flattened area of the dome around the *oculus* was entirely made of pumice stone.

The Symbolism of the Pantheon

What was the significance of this religious space? First, the Pantheon was clearly no ordinary temple. Instead of a rectangular *cella* containing a statue of the god, it presented a vast internal space, forming a large meeting place whose nature implied an upsurge of ceremonial and ancient ritual. Second, this space displays particular specifications: the ground plan is circular, with the height of the inner cylinder equivalent to the radius of the plan; the dome, of the same diameter, is a true hemisphere. Consequently, the internal space could contain a perfect sphere, enclosed in a cube whose sides measure twice the length of the radius. Finally, if we prolong the measurement of the base into the back of the apses, an equilateral triangle can be traced from the ground to the center of the *oculus* above, to form a perfect pyramid.

All these geometrical configurations were considered by the ancients to be invested with numerical and symbolic significance that made the monument a veritable Pythagorean entity. A text by Cicero comes to mind (*The Nature of the Gods*, II, 47):

"You say that a cone or a cylinder or a pyramid seems to you more beautiful than a sphere. Let us suppose these other shapes are more beautiful, in appearance at least, although I do not think so. For what can be more beautiful than the shape which alone contains and includes all others? A shape which has in it no irregularity, nothing to offend, no sharp angles, no bends, no protrusions, no concavity or deficiency of any kind? There are in fact two preeminent shapes: among solids, the solid globe or "sphere" (*sphaera*) as it is called in Greek, and among plane figures, the round or orb, or "circle" (*kyklos*) as the Greeks would say... No other shape [than the sphere] could preserve such uniformity of motion and regularity in orbit."

These solids are an expression of divine intelligence: from the square to the cube, from the circle to the cylinder, from the pyramid to the cone, all shapes converge in the sphere.

This fundamental geometry always returned to the image of the universe and the movement of the celestial bodies. The Pantheon is a perfect example. In the hall, the seven apses are dedicated to the seven astral divinities (five planets and two luminaries, Sol and Luna – the sun and the moon). The dome itself represented the celestial vault. The five coffered levels of the ceiling symbolize the five concentric spheres of the planetary system according to the ancients. The central *oculus* – sole source of light for the building, admirably represented the sun, which dominated the whole space. Like the emperor who reigned over the *orbis terrarum*, holding in one hand the globe of the universe and wearing the crown of rays, it was the image of the *sol divinus*, the divine sun that would become the *sol invictus*.

The Pantheon, dynastic temple and symbol of the princeps' power, was the place where sovereign was transformed into universal legislator. It was here, according to Dion Cassius, that Hadrian chose to "lay down the law" among the gods. It was here that the all-powerful emperor proclaimed legal doctrine, promulgated the laws, and became the head of the supreme court. He had built a temple in the image of deified imperial power itself, the *aula regia* par excellence.

Page 159 top
Detail of the ceiling coffers
Note the subtlety of the displacement toward the top of the strengthening elements in order to correct the optical distortion due to the observer's position on the ground and not at the level of the hemisphere. The five levels of these coffers correspond to the five layers that make up the homocentric heaven of the planets. A star of gilt bronze was placed in the center of each of these 112 coffers.

Page 159 bottom
Flawless stylistic discipline
Detail of a triangular pediment above the blind bays on the upper level of the Pantheon.

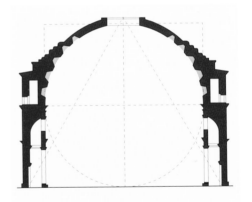

Reflection of mystic theory
Relating to the mystic of number and geometrical forms, the Pantheon reveals numerous aspects that explain its spatial perfection. The cylindrical building is contained within a square that contains a circle (or a sphere within a cube). In addition, an equilateral triangle links the *oculus* to the opposing apses, forming the shape of a cone or the angles of a pyramid.

Hadrian's Villa

The Pantheon represents a grandiose, bold urban project, embodying a dynastic sanctuary of striking originality and rich symbolic meaning. The work that Hadrian envisaged for his palace, the *Villa Hadriana* near Tivoli, gave him the opportunity to express his personality in a totally different direction: that of architecture integrated with landscape.

Like many other Roman emperors, Hadrian chose to build his palace outside Rome. In the *urbs*, material limitations (lack of space) combined with ethical and political considerations (the old Republican spirit that still subsisted) limited his ambitions. At Tivoli, a day's horse ride from the capital, the ruler could give his imagination a free rein regarding the conceptual and emblematic character of the buildings.

At the foot of the hills of ancient Tibur, the sovereign built his palatial villa on land belonging to the family of his wife, Sabina, in splendid woodland countryside, irrigated by numerous streams flowing down the Annio valley. In 118, work was started on the construction of a vast building program stretching more than 1200 meters from north to south and more than 600 meters from east to west. The buildings scattered in the countryside cover 66 hectares. All around, the undulating meadows and forests stretch as far as the eye can see. On a clear day, it is possible to glimpse the Frascati vineyards and the hills of Albano at the foot of the Praenestine mountains.

This rural landscape serves as a setting for a palatial complex amidst magnificent gardens. In that place Hadrian developed a similar formula to Nero's Domus Aurea, magnifying it to the scale of the land available. He adopted a program inspired by the *paradeisoi* of the Parthian and Hellenistic rulers. Grottoes, a pool, fountains, waterfalls, fishponds, and lakes reflecting the buildings scattered freely among the greenery, flower beds, and plantations all contributed to this

Hadrian's Villa

General plan of the central zone of the *Villa Hadriana* at Tivoli. This imperial palace that Hadrian built from A.D. 118 comprises some 30 buildings:

1. Theater
2. *Tholos* of Venus
3. Terrace of the Temple
4. Guest accommodation
5. Latin library; 6. Greek library
7. Republican villa
8. Library courtyard
9. Teatro Marittimo
10. Hall of the Philosophers
11. Poikile-Hippodrome
12. Courtyard of the winter palace
13. Heliocaminus; 14. Piazza d'Oro
15. Doric pilasters; 16. Barracks
17. Portico of the fish ponds
18. Garden-stadium
19. Three-*exedra* casino
20. Lesser baths
21. Vestibule
22. Greater baths
23. Praetorium
24. *Canopus*
25. Temple of Serapis
26. Tower of Roccabruna
27. Academy
28. Temple of Jupiter

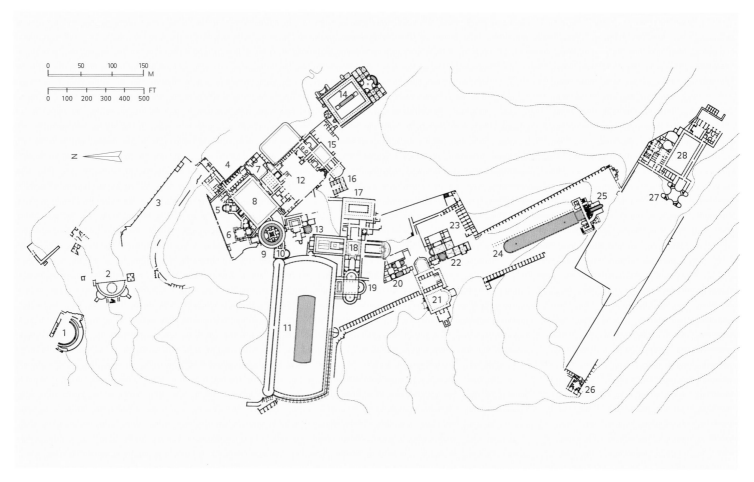

Innovative masterpiece
Model of Hadrian's Villa in Tivoli: the area of the Teatro Marittimo and the libraries, including the Piazza d'Oro, the courtyard of the Doric pilasters and in the background the Hippodrome with its central *euripus*.

prodigious ensemble of Hadrian's Villa, with its animal reserves, aviary, and game park. Between the periods that Hadrian dedicated to his grand tours around the empire, the building site was as busy as a beehive. Occasionally on the return of the architect emperor, certain parts that did not satisfy his design had to be demolished. In no respect was the architecture imposing or pompous. The scale of the home of this deified emperor remained completely human.

Every detail was calculated to provide extraordinary comfort and luxury. In order to enjoy peace and quiet, Hadrian decided that horse-drawn carriages would use a system of underground roads. Consequently, the various groups of buildings, theater, *tholos* of Venus, hippodrome (*poikile*), *triclinium*, libraries, guest accommodation, winter palace, Piazza d'Oro, Teatro Marittimo, barracks, cryptoporticoes, stadium, greater and lesser baths, *canopus* and Sanctuary of Serapis, Academy and Temple of Jupiter, all were freely distributed in the landscape. The scheme had no orthogonal ground plan, no central focus, and no dominant orientation. Everything was dictated by imagination and spontaneity. As a result, a great variety of styles, techniques, forms and structures exist at Hadrian's Villa. Although it was pillaged and vandalized from late antiquity onward, especially during the Renaissance, the site has not yet yielded all its riches. At present, a third of the buildings, in particular in the southern area of the site, have not yet been systematically excavated. It would be premature to attempt a global reading of the imperial intentions embodied by this palace. Only certain edifices can be interpreted at present to give an indication of the great importance and rich semiological content of the site as a whole.

The Role of the Palace Site

The role of these multiple building groups remains difficult to determine. Since antiquity, various authors have proposed different explanations: it could be the "chronicle of a journey" (according to Spartian) or the emperor might have been indulging his version of a "Great Exhibition" or "a garden of marvels," or "follies" in the manner of those created by Ludwig II of Bavaria. Such explanations are somewhat simplistic, however. The intention was profoundly different and more complex. It has already been shown that palaces played a crucial role in court ritual and religious worship. It would seem that beyond the necessities of shelter and the daily life of a considerable household, Hadrian's Villa consisted of a series of buildings intended to express the various facets of the emperor and the roles he assumed from a religious point of view.

Since the Hellenistic period, sovereigns have adopted all sorts of divine attributes. In certain temples, the king was the *synnaos*, or the companion of the god worshipped in the *naos*. He was present in person or in the form of a religious statue. He claimed affinities with various gods. For these reasons, he bore the names of Soter (saviour like Zeus), Olympieios (olympic like Jupiter), Kallinikos (victorious like Heracles), or Aulete (flute player like Apollo). In place of the gods, he was Epiphanes (marking his presence as god apparent), Evergetes (doer of good deeds), Nicator the victor, and so forth. He personified Neos-Dionysos and symbolized the chosen one of Fortuna, of Tyche, to which he owed his stature of divine victor. He was the *cosmocrator* who compared himself to the immortals like Jupiter, Hercules, and Helios. So for each one of these divine roles that a sovereign could assume according to his situation, Hadrian had wanted a place specially dedicated to a particular type of worship, with suitable outward appearances and surroundings.

Page 163
The *tholos* of Venus
Among the exemplary sanctuaries of Hadrian's Villa, the *tholos* of Venus reproduces a Doric design inspired from classical Greece. The curvilinear forms illustrate Hadrian's architectural experimentation.

An *exedra* in the greater baths of Hadrian's Villa
The structures of the thermal halls are built by means of vaults made of thin layers of concrete.

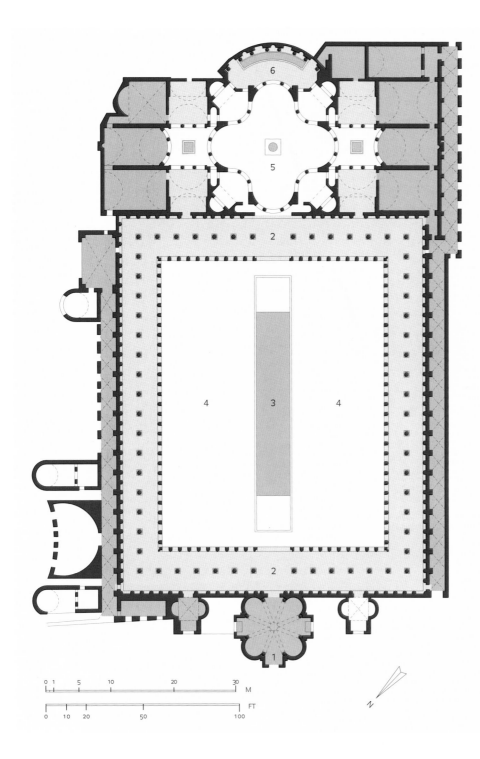

Plan of the Piazza d'Oro
This is one of the most difficult components of the imperial complex to interpret. The "trefoil" area was initially visualized with vaulting. It was later noticed that the structure was too weak to support a solid roof.
1. Entrance with octagonal ribbed vault
2. Double portico forming a peristyle
3. Central pool
4. Courtyard-garden
5. Mixtilinear hypethral hall (open air)
6. Exedral nymphaeum

The Sacred Places

The diversity of the various palace buildings at the *Villa Hadriana* is the most striking feature. It marks a trend that was to culminate in the Great Palace of Justinian (565) at Constantinople, with its sequence of buildings designed for the court liturgy as described by Constantine VII Porphyrogenitus (around 940) in his *De ceremoniis*: the Augusteion, the palace of the Magnaura, the imperial palace and Enneadekacubita (banquet hall of the nineteen couches), the phiale of the Triconchos, the Triconchos, the Chrysotriclinos, the Cathisma. In the same way, the palace of Tivoli had its Temple of Venus, its Piazza d'Oro, its Teatro Marittimo, its *triclinium* with three *exedras*, its *canopus*, its Temple of Serapis, its Temple of Jupiter.

If the modern names of the sites of Hadrian's Villa do not necessarily correspond to the original designation of the buildings, each edifice had a particular role in the context of the court ritual. Was this a radical departure from the historical context? No, according to Louis Bréhier, who says that the "Byzantine institutions actually represent an organic development of the Roman State." He adds, "Rome bequeathed to Byzantium the providential character of the imperial state, the adoration and the deification of the emperor's person, as well as the absolute power of the sovereign." The multiplication of the locations connected to the different phases of imperial worship and to the roles of the sovereign in the context of court liturgy did not suddenly appear at Constantinople; it had been developing with the Hellenistic kings and flourished during the Hadrianic period. A complex such as Hadrian's Villa constitutes perhaps the best illustration of the modalities of imperial religion. Its culmination in the West (293–305), represented by the palace at Piazza Armerina (Sicily, early fourth century) passed on the tradition, and this ritual found a new lease of life at the Byzantine court of Constantinople, surviving in the Eastern Empire.

The Sanctuaries of Dionysos and Serapis

Amid the restored sites of Hadrian's Villa, excavation was carried out during the 1950s on the *canopus* and the sanctuary of Serapis, as well as on the Teatro Marittimo and then, around 1970, on the Piazza d'Oro. This last site, situated to the east of the palace, constitutes one of the most unusual constructions ever built in the Roman world. It is the culmination of curvilinear Hadrianic architecture. The whole formed a vast rectangle 100 meters by 60 meters on a northeast-southwest axis. A triple entrance gave access to a courtyard surrounded on its four sides (46 by 37 meters) by a double portico with a central pool. At the back of the courtyard was the sanctuary in the form of a nymphaeum. This was a hypethral (open-air) structure on a centered cruciform ground plan, whose sinuous outline was contained within an octagon. The "undulating" colonnade, with curved architraves on marble Corinthian columns, delineated an area whose limits were either concave (on the central axes) or convex (on the diagonal), with squinches in the corners. Situated on either side of the central trefoil-shaped structure were small, vaulted rooms surrounding a square pool. At the back of the complex, a quarter-circle constituted the nymphaeum. Its curved wall contained seven grotto-work niches flanked by colonnettes, with a correspondingly curved pool situated in front. It had an abundant supply of water, thanks to an aqueduct visible at the back of the structure, that fed the cascades, the water spouts, and the fountains, before flowing into a series of pools that converged on the central "canal."

This curious and elegant structure, of ethereal grace and fluid lines, was designed for the worship of Dionysos, often in relation to the nymphs, with the addition of the characters of Ariadne, Silenus, satyrs, Maenads, and Bacchae, forming the Bacchic *thiasos*. Hadrian, imbued with Greek culture, officially promoted the cult of Dionysos. In 123 at Ancyra (Ankara), the emperor had organized a mystical *agon* (a religious assembly) placed under the direction of the imperial synod. He appeared at it in the person of Neos-Dionysos, according to the Hellenistic tradition. In 125 and 132, he officiated at the major Dionysan festivals at Athens. At Teos (headquarters of the society of Dionysan artists), he consecrated a temple that associated Dionysos and Antinous. At Ephesus, he organized a Dionysan procession that revived the procession of Ptolemy II Philadelphos at Alexandria in 271 B.C., described by Atheneus. Hadrian, in the guise of Dionysos, was worshipped there. In these ways, he helped spread the influence of Hellenic cults in the Roman world.

The same approach governed the creation of the *canopus* of Hadrian's Villa, whose pool, 119 by 18 meters, led to the sanctuary of Serapis. The name *canopus* evokes the canal built at Alexandria between the Canopic Nile and the famous sanctuary dedicated to the Graeco-Egyptian god. At the entrance of this splendid

Two figures of Silenus flank the caryatids
The group of caryatids along the edge of the *canopus* of the Serapeum at Hadrian's Villa. The themes of Hellenic art illustrate Hadrian's passion for Greek culture.

pool, lying in the fold of a small valley, stands a semicircular portico. Under this colonnade, decorated with an alternately straight and arched frieze, stand the statues of Mars, Mercury, and Minerva. On the right, four caryatids, replicas of those on the Erechtheion at Athens, flanked by two Silenus figures supported a pergola that was reflected in the water. Finally, at the southern end of the canal, the Serapeum was built into the hillside. Its decoration with sculptures of Ptah, Isis, and Osiris underscored the Alexandrian origin of the god. The sanctuary in the shape of a large exedra covered by a concrete vault partly prefigures the triconchos of the Great Palace of Constantinople. It has the appearence of a huge semicircular iwan mesuring 22 meters in diameter (75 feet, the equivalent of the radius of the Pantheon), with a very complex semicircular structure at the back,

Page 167

Delicate porticoes and statuary
The colonnade borders the far end of the *canopus* at Hadrian's Villa. In a scheme unique to Hadrianic architecture, alternating lintels and arches in the curvilinear porticoes create a truly baroque style.

In memory of Alexandria
View of the *canopus* at Hadrian's Villa. The reference to the Canopic canal of the Nile was an allusion to the cult of Serapis.

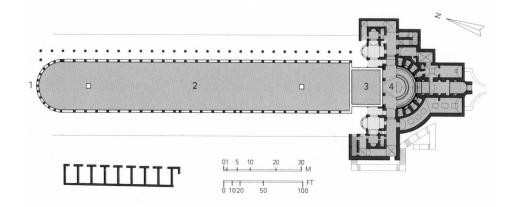

A Nilotic Serapeum at Tivoli
General plan of the *canopus* at Hadrian's Villa.
1. Mixtilinear portico with statues
2. Large pool
3. Entrance pool
4. Temple of Serapis

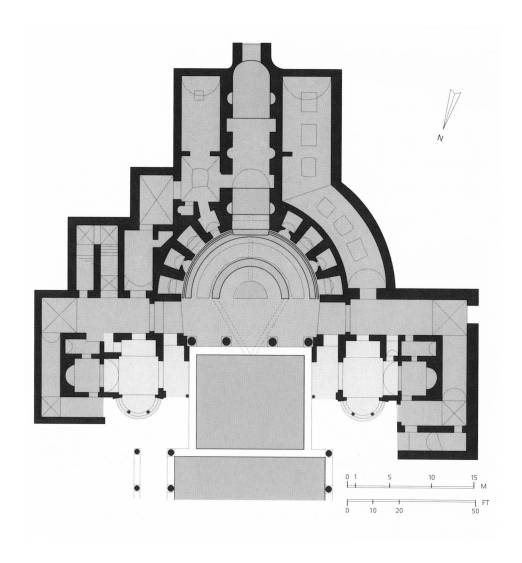

Plan of the Temple of Serapis
The semi-subterranean complex structure of the sanctuary of Serapis, with its concentric pools and artificial grotto, is an example of Hadrianic art at its peak.

connected to the canal by a series of underground pools. Here there is an apse, surrounded by eight niches flanking an artificial grotto approximately 20 meters deep. From this grotto-nymphaeum, with its concentric pools, the sound of cascades echoed inside a succession of peripheral vaulted chambers. At the back of this dark, quasi-subterranean cave, with water all about, the atmosphere was conducive to the presence of the chthonian god, ruler of the dead, now honored, in his incarnation of the nocturnal sun, as the image of the resurrection.

Serapis had already been revered by Nero. Domitian had built a Serapeum to him in the Campus Martius. Depicted in the *forma urbis*, its plan shows similarities to the Tivoli sanctuary. Hadrian himself built the Serapeum of Alexandria. A commemorative coin shows the emperor as *synnaos* of Serapis, the two standing together beneath a canopy topped with a pediment. Here he was effectively *Neos-Serapis*, wielding power over the afterlife.

The different sanctuaries of court ritual present at Hadrian's Villa are many: the portico of Doric pilasters with its basilical hall; the so-called Academy, whose curvilinear plan is as complex as the Piazza d'Oro; the temple of Venus with its *tholos* built into a semicircular portico; the Temple of Jupiter and its circular hall. The cosmological significance of the *poikile*-Hippodrome deserves mention, with its *euripe* (central pool) in the place of the *spina*, and its *cathisma* (imperial box), from where the emperor watched the two- and four-horse chariot races, whose course was supposed to represent the stars' movements in the arena of the sky.

Grotto of the Graeco-Egyptian God

Built against the hill and forming a vast concrete-covered *exedra*, the Sanctuary of Serapis, at the farthest end of the *canopus*, is a place of chthonian worship at Hadrian's Villa. A system of concentric canals and rooms that penetrate deep into the hill formed the stage for initiation ceremonies.

The Role of the Teatro Marittimo

Above all, the infinitely complex, mysterious structure of the so-called Teatro Marittimo, between the Hall of the Philosophers and the Greek and Latin libraries, draws attention because of its rich emblematic and semiological meaning.

On an architectural level, the Teatro Marittimo is the most original creation of Hadrian's Villa. Its ground plan consists of a series of concentric structures. A tetrastyle vestibule leads to the main structure, which is surrounded by a cylindrical wall of brick 9 meters high enclosing a hypethral area, for the most part open to the sky. The diameter of this "enclosure" is 150 feet (44 meters, like the rotunda of the Pantheon). Inside, a covered walkway runs around the building in the form of a circular portico, 4 meters wide, supported by 40 marble Ionic columns. This peristyle is covered by a circular vault supported on one side by the cylindrical wall and on the other by the colonnade.

The water of a circular moat, 4 meters wide, laps the base of the colonnade. It surrounds an islet, 27 meters in diameter, on which various buildings stand, in particular, a central pavilion with marble fluted columns. This four-pillared canopy is formed out of concave porticoes. A lens-shaped *exedra* preceded it on the side of the entrance hall. Placed on the central axis, this *exedra* is surrounded by two curvilinear colonnades. Various additions, in particular, tiny baths and rooms conforming to the configuration dictated by the curved ground plan, constitute what amounts to a miniature house covering the island.

Two movable wooden bridges allowed access from the covered walk to the central island. They were revolving walkways on wheels, remains of which have been found at the bottom of the moat. These bridges were situated on the right and left of the entrance and allowed access to either end of the *exedra*. There was therefore no central access.

Teatro Marittimo
The portico surrounding the circular moat of the Teatro Marittimo at Hadrian's Villa. The 40 Ionic columns reflect themselves in the waters that isolate the central island, which is accessible by movable wooden bridges. In the background appears the superstructure of the Greek library.

Circular colonnade
Covered by a curved vault, the portico of the Teatro Marittimo rests, on one side, on the cylindrical exterior wall and, on the other, on the colonnade at the edge of the moat. The whole is governed by a centripetal scheme.

What was this mysterious construction, built entirely of curves, circular shapes, curvilinear vaults and colonnades, successive concentric circles, a circular moat, an isolated central island, unconnected with the rest of the palace complex? To date, various hypotheses have been formulated to explain the role of this building. Some thought it was a *natatio*, or swimming pool; others construed it as an "ivory tower" where the reputedly misanthropic or hypochondriac emperor could take refuge far from the world to meditate in peace. But would such trivial needs have necessitated such a profusion of formal and architectural innovations?

In order to understand the meaning of this sacred place forming the *ombilicos* of Hadrian's Villa, reference must be made to Varro's Aviary, a famous prototype of this complex design. This building, 170 years older than the Teatro Marittimo of Hadrian's Villa, stood on the grounds at Casinum belonging to the Latin encyclopedist Terentius Varro (116–127 B.C.) who describes it in detail in his *Res rusticae* (see text and plan on page 180).

A reading of this curious text reveals great similarities between Varro's Aviary and Hadrian's Teatro Marittimo: both have a round structure and a circular colonnaded walk surrounding a moat with an islet in its center, where a canopied *tholos* stood.

The conceptual analogy between these two buildings has been noted by various commentators. As early as the Renaissance, the architect Pirro Ligorio (1513–1583) pointed out this connection with engravings showing a reconstruction of the aviary. Nevertheless, historians apparently did not heed the series of essential details supplied by Varro that allow us to grasp the true function of the supposed aviary and the Teatro Marittimo. The wealth of technological features mentioned by Varro is understandably surprising if the building under discussion were really a simple aviary.

General view of the concentric
structure of the Teatro Marittimo
In the center, the circular islet was
used for court ritual. The diameter
of the complex is identical to that
of the Pantheon: 150 Roman feet.

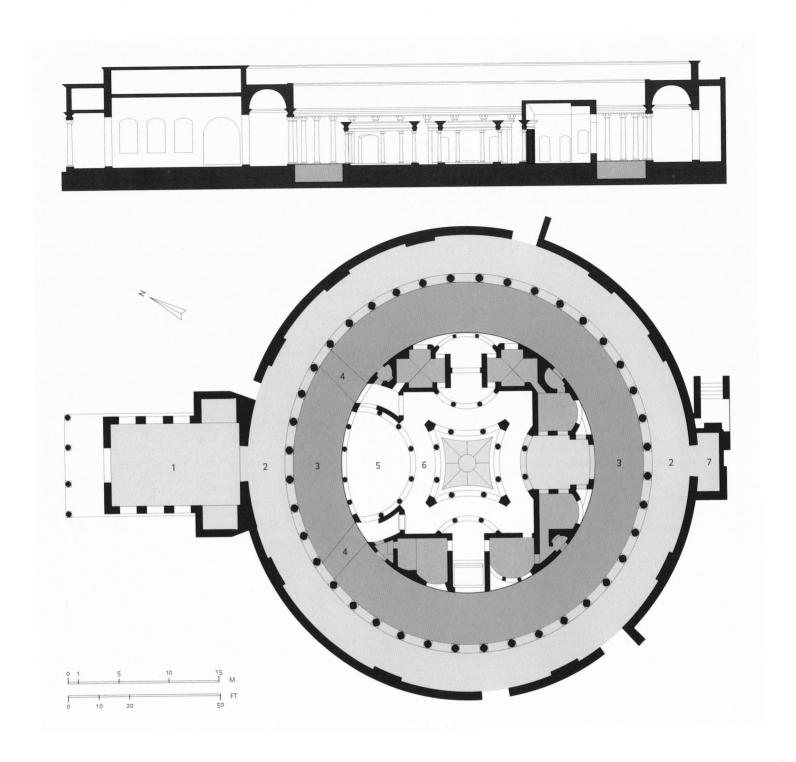

Indeed, in his description, the author refers to couches of a *triclinium*, a table in the form of a wheel supplying water through taps, a weather vane on top of the central dome linked to an arrow inside the cupola by which one could tell the direction of the wind without leaving the *tholos*. Finally he mentions an extraordinary mechanism: two stars (Lucifer and Vesper) rotate around the cupola, indicating the time both day and night. (For further details, refer to my account published in both *Hadrien et l'architecture romaine [Hadrian and Roman Architecture]*, 1984, and in *L'Astrologie et le pouvoir [Astrology and Power]*, 1986.) Here, it will suffice to summarize the results of a meticulous analysis that, paradoxically, concludes that Varro's supposed aviary had a cosmological-astrological role. In this, the building relates closely to the *coenatio* of Nero's Domus Aurea, taking its place within a whole series of creations intended to reflect a representation of the cosmos and to facilitate the consultation of the stars with a view to interpreting signs in order to predict the future, a preoccupation of the ancients.

Section and plan of the Teatro Marittimo at Tivoli
1. Entrance; 2. Circular portico
3. Moat; 4. Movable bridges
5. *Pronaos;* 6. Central canopy
7. Apse

Page 175
Real and virtual elements combine
The white marble columns of the Ionic portico dominate the waters of the circular moat in the Teatro Marittimo at Tivoli.

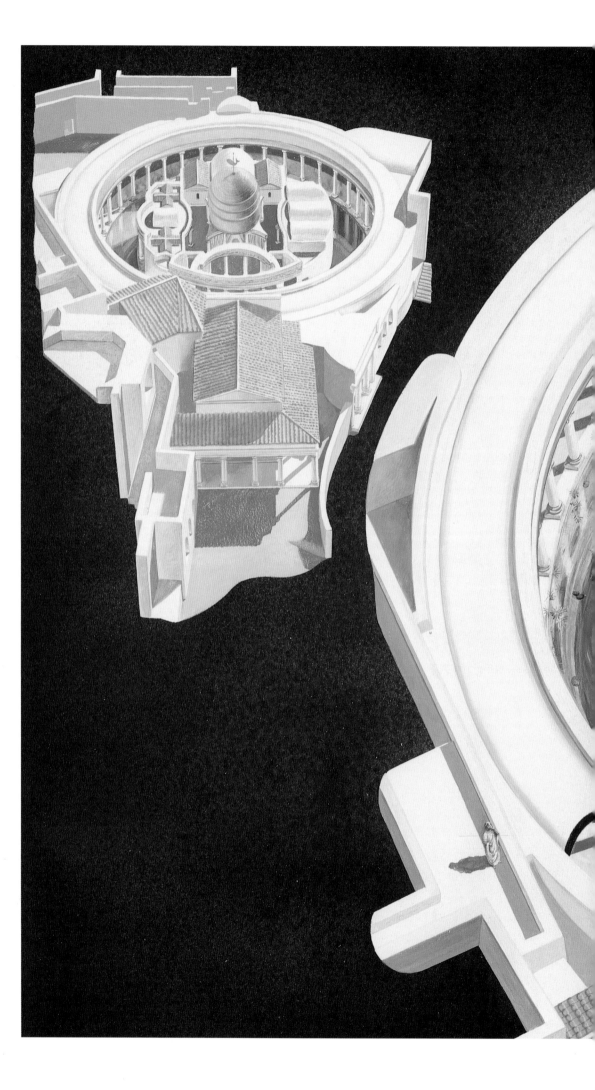

A center for astral divination

Left

Reconstruction of the Teatro Marittimo at Hadrian's Villa, showing the circular composition with the round islet with its domed canopy.

Right

Open reconstruction of the Teatro Marittimo at Hadrian's Villa. In the radioconcentric space, the architect designed a microcosm, with its diverse elements and natural worlds – vegetable and animal. The circular structure reproduced the ancient image of the world according to Strabo and Claudius Ptolemy. As in Varro's Aviary, fish swam in the moat and birds flew in a netted area, they represented the fauna of this *imago mundi*. On the central islet, the *pronaos* stands in front of the astral domed canopy, where the court ritual and consultations of the horoscope took place.

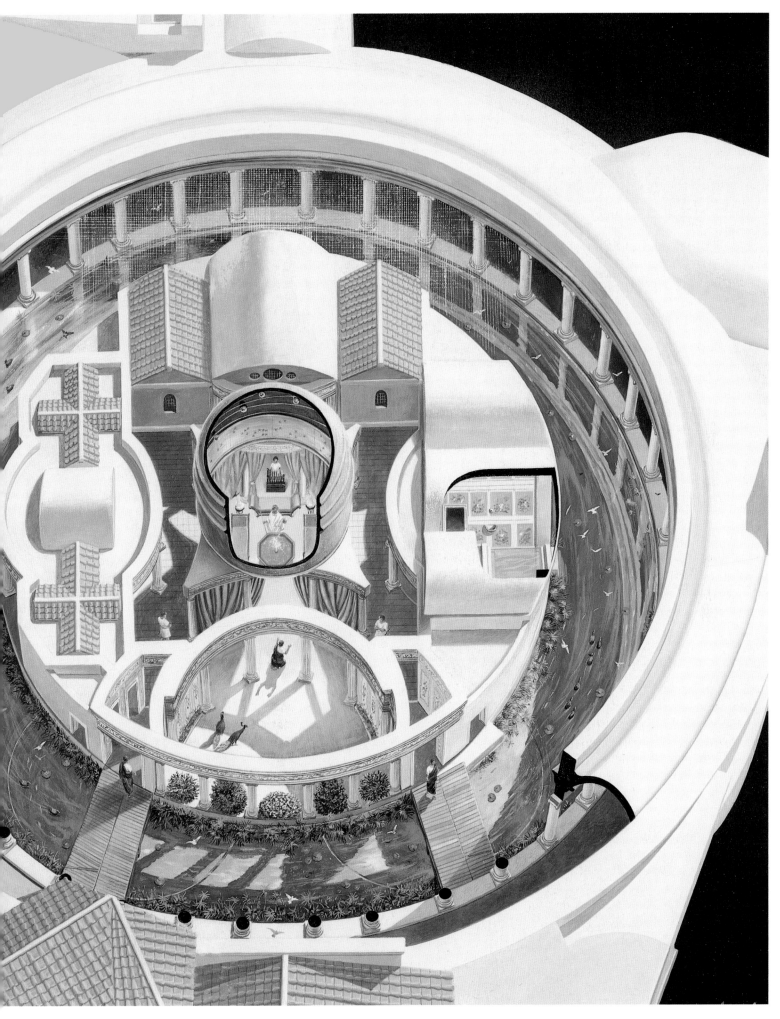

Returning to the plan of the two buildings, the scheme is as follows: The circular moat represents, in ancient cosmology, the primordial ocean surrounding the earth; the round islet is the *oikoumene* (the inhabited world), according to Strabo's geography (58 B.C.–A.D. 25); the cupola of the *tholos* symbolizes the sky, with the ceaseless movements of the stars; the whole concentric construction reflects the ancient concept of the universe made up of spheres contained within each other.

Varro's universe in miniature (microcosm) was a representation of the various animal, vegetable, and mineral kingdoms: the walkway and island were inhabited by man; the water of the moat contains fish (aquarium); the air was the domain of the birds (some of which made the transition from air to water, such as the ducks, which were specifically mentioned); moreover, the plumbing system allowed control of the water and thus the power to make rain fall, as in the Domus Aurea; finally, the mechanism of the cupola reproduced the movements of the planets and the stars, and the weather vane indicated the direction of the wind, which, according to ancient beliefs, propelled the astral movements and influenced the horoscope. Moreover, the *triclinium* can be compared, according to H. P. L'Orange, to a throne room.

Such was the emblematic "machinery" of Varro's aviary for the purpose of divination. For indeed, as in the grotto of Tiberius at Sperlonga, the fishes in the aquarium were used for ichthyomancy, the birds for ornithomancy, and the installation in the form of a planetarium for astrology, the whole housed within a representation of the world. This aviary was not only an *imago mundi* but, on a miniature scale, one of those *paradaisoi* dear to the Parthian and Hellenistic rulers in the east.

Thus, in concluding that the Teatro Marittimo was an *aula regia* in the image of the universe, one must suppose that there probably existed, above the central canopy occupying the middle of the islet, a cupola, probably made out of bronze, containing a planetarium mechanism that enabled the consultation of the horoscope. It is here that the emperor, whose passion for astrology is well known, consulted the heavens. And it was also here that he appeared in the *exedra*, according to the ritual of the sovereign Epiphanes, in all the glory of a living god. It was here that he appeared as master of the world, the *cosmocrator*.

An analysis of Varro's text leads to a reinterpretation of the Teatro Marittimo and confers on it an essential role in the process of imperial deification in Hadrian's time.

In architectural terms, Hadrian's Villa constitutes an unrivaled repertory of new solutions and forms. There the creator's vision of extreme freedom and exceptional originality can be seen. This palace represents the *summum* of curvilinear design expressed in works full of grace and lightness. These Hadrianic sanctuaries and pavilions were always conceived on a human scale, a characteristic that makes the palace of Tivoli a fitting complement to the huge, powerful space of the Pantheon.

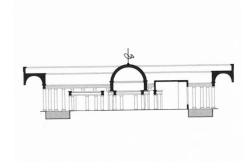

Dome
Reconstituted section of the Teatro Marittimo at Hadrian's Villa, with a dome over the central canopy.

Page 179
Ciborium
In the middle of the Teatro Marittimo, marble traces survive of the canopied pavilion, which originally consisted of four pillars and eight columns. One must suppose the existence, on top of this structure, of a dome with an astronomical function, in all likelihood constructed in metal. On ground level was a throne and a *triclinium*, as well as a fountain with water spouts fed by a water conduit whose traces were discovered by archaeologists under the islet and the circular moat.

Gods beneath a canopy

Sketch of a painting from Pompeii, in the House of Apollo, discovered in 1839. The work represents a canopy with fine colonnettes, with Bacchus and Venus (?) on either side of Apollo in the guise of *cosmocrator*, enthroned under the central dome.

Varro's Aviary:
A Prototype of the Teatro Marittimo

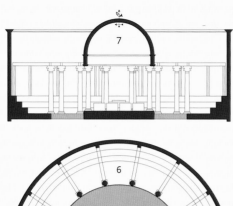

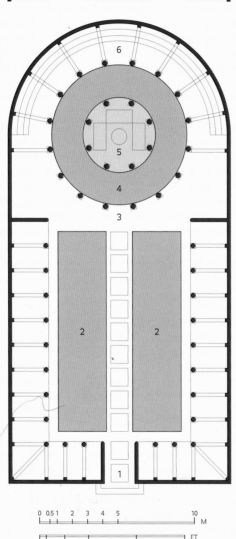

The passage that follows, dating from around 45/40 B.C., by the Latin author Terentius Varro, describes the aviary that he owned at Casinum, (*Res Rusticae*, Book III, chapter 5):

"This aviary is enclosed by high walls right and left. The shape of it is like that of a writing tablet with a rounded top. The rectangular area is 48 feet wide (14 meters) and 72 feet long (21 meters), with the rounded area measuring 27 feet (8 meters). At the rectangular end, and a door leads to a courtyard.

On each side are rows of stone columns. These colonnades are covered with netting and filled with all kinds of birds. In the open quadrangle are two fish ponds and between them a path leading to a domed colonnaded building. This round building is circled by a promenade 5 feet (1.5 meters) wide, beyond which a thicket of trees can be seen.

The round building has one row of stone columns and in the middle a second row of wooden columns. The outer columns are surrounded with fine netting; the interior columns are also enclosed with a net. In between the two rows of columns there is a kind of bird theater built of perches attached to the columns. All kinds of birds, especially songbirds, are kept inside.

The paving stones on which the columns stand are edged with a stone border that forms a 2 foot (60 cm) high boundary with the 1 foot (30 cm) deep, ring-shaped pool. Ducks swim on the water around the central island which serves as the basis for the *tholos* formed by the central ring of wooden columns already mentioned. In the middle of this building there is a spoked wheel for a revolving table, and cold and warm water can be turned on for the guests from taps on the table.

The wooden columned pavilion is crowned by a dome in which the morning and evening stars (Lucifer and Vesper) revolve and show the time. On top of the dome there is also a compass of the eight winds like that in the Tower of Winds at Athens. It is equipped with an arrow that indicates which way the wind is blowing, so that one can tell which way it is blowing without having to go outside the pavilion."

Section and plan of the so-called Aviary of Varro, reconstructed according to the description given by the author:
1. Entrance
2. Fish ponds
3. Circular wooden colonnade, surrounding the pool
4. Circular pool
5. Islet bearing the marble *tholos* with its *triclinium*
6. "Theater" for the birds
7. Cupola crowning the central *tholos* topped by a weathervane

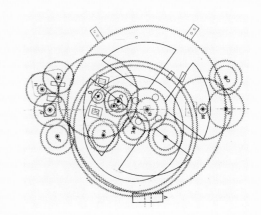

An astronomical "computer"
Diagram of the bronze mechanism of Antikythera (circa 90–87 B.C.), such as Derek de Solla Price reconstructed it, with cogwheels of varying dimensions and complex gearing. The astronomical instrument had a divination function, relating to the horoscope, and enabled one to establish the position of the planets.

The Mechanisms of Antiquity

Such a description of a mechanism capable of making stars rotate on the firmament of a cupola forming a sort of planetarium might surprise the reader. The study of ancient texts shows, however, that many authors tackled the subject; there is no lack of written accounts. Thus, in the *Republic* (Book I, XIV, 21–22), Cicero describes a sphere constructed by Archimedes that reproduced the "rotation of bodies according to irregular and various orbits, at different speeds." It represented the course of the planets and determined the constellations of solar and lunar eclipses. Cicero was so impressed that he resumed his account in *Tusculanes* (I, XXV, 61). In his treatise entitled *The Nature of the Gods* (II, XXXIV–XXXV), he indicated that another philosopher-engineer, Posidonius of Apameus, had created a similar instrument. Many other texts could be quoted. But for a long time, historians maintained that these were poetic fictions, denying any technological expertise in the Graeco-Roman world.

Recently, however, they have begun to accept that mechanical systems did exist in Hellenistic and Roman times, due to the discovery of a crucial piece of evidence proving without doubt the presence of mechanical expertise in antiquity. It is not a text but rather an irrefutable piece of material evidence: a Hellenistic bronze mechanism. Built in Rhodes around 90 B.C., it is known by the name of the Antikythera mechanism, because it was recovered in 1900 by fishermen from a wreck sunk between the Matapan cape and the island of Antikythera.

This discovery nevertheless had to wait until 1974 and the studies of Derek de Solla Price of Yale University to emerge from obscurity. This mechanism, corroded by its 2000 years in the sea, measures 32 by 17 by 10 centimeters. It comprises 30 cogs with teeth ranging from 15 to 225 in number. Its outer casing bears an inscription, of which 793 letters have been deciphered; the text derives from the Isagogus of Geminos, a Stoic of the school of Posidonius, and concerns astrometeorology, with mention of the names of the constellations, the signs of the zodiac, and the dates of the solstices and equinoxes. This mechanism reproduced the composition of the sky at any time of the past, present, or future. A hypothesis not entertained by Derek de Solla Price is that this was a "computer" before its time, intended for the scrutiny of the heavens for horoscopic purposes.

In confirmation of this interpretation, reference should be made to the Greek poet Nonnos of Pannopolis who in the fifth century A.D. wrote the *Dionysiacs* (VI, 1–104). He shows that it was usual to refer to such instruments in antiquity. An astrologer called Astraios, elaborating an astral theme, takes from a box "a revolving sphere, a perfect globe, image of the heavens, reflection of the universe," and then "made one end revolve on its axis, setting the heavens in motion." Thus this "make-believe celestial vault of artificial stars turns unceasingly around its pole."

Varro's Aviary (*Aviarum Varonis*) reconstructed by Pirro Ligorio in 1581
In rediscovering antiquity, the Renaissance was haunted by ancient writing on architecture. The description of the aviary fired the imagination.

The Roman Cities of Tunisia

By submitting the rich Tunisian region from 146 B.C. onward to a rigorous program of centuriation in units of land measuring 710 meters square, Rome demonstrated its determination to subject the region to rational development. The conquered territory was the object of remarkable capital investment. Roads, aqueducts, bridges, dams, cisterns, and drainage schemes were undertaken as the new cities began to develop. For example, in order to supply Carthage with water, a reservoir was built at Djebel Zaghouan with an impressive *templum aquis* (Temple of the Waters), and 70 kilometers of canal was built in the form of an aqueduct on arcades to supply water to the city and its ports.

In the northwest of the country, Bulla Regia contains an interesting architectural variant adapted to the climate. In order to avoid the intense heat of the summer, the owners of urban homes duplicated the ground floor living rooms in the basement. Consequently, under the ruins visible at street level, the under-

Arches alternate with architraves
The spare industrial-style architecture of Brisgane resorts to powerful arches, created with the help of huge archstones. At mid-height, the presence of ogee molding shows that functionalism did not exclude all aesthetic preoccupations.

A center of olive production
Only the bare framework structure of the main hall of agricultural production of Brisgane survives today. Between the monolithic pillars and lintels, a rubble stonework filling covered the walls.

Temple of the Waters at Zaghouan
At the entrance of the Temple of the Waters at Zaghouan (Ziqua), in the mountain range situated to the south of Tunis, a curious nymphaeum, with its figure-of-eight-shaped pool at the foot of the sacred terrace. A spring fed the aqueduct, which supplied Carthage, 70 kilometers north, with drinking water. This sanctuary dates from Hadrian's era, around A.D. 130.

ground apartments intended for the summer season stand intact. These contain porticuses and luxurious adaptations. It was here, in these cellars, lit by the well of light from the two-story atrium, that life was conducted during the torrid summer heat. Such an arrangement exists in the House of Amphitrite, which is decorated with a fine floor mosaic depicting Venus emerging from the sea, and it demonstrates the ingenuity of the builders in the second and third centuries A.D.

The city of Dougga, situated farther to the south in a region of rugged hills, has a superb capitol built around 166. The hexastyle temple, its high fluted columns and Corinthian capitals turned golden by years of strong sunlight, numbers among the most remarkable monuments of Roman Africa. From the top of a flight of stairs, the podium overlooks the terraced forum dominating a grandiose landscape. The depiction of an apotheosis (that of Antoninus Pius) decorating its pediment demonstrates that imperial deification in connection with Iuppiter Optimus Maximus.

To the west, a sanctuary dedicated to Juno Caelestis, a reincarnation of the goddess Tanit, symbol of the moon and fertility, who was venerated by the Carthaginians, was built around 225, during the time of the emperor Severus Alexander. The building stands within a large hemicycle consisting of a semicircular porticus of 24 columns. This design obviously refers to the celestial vault and to the twenty-four hours of the daily astral cycle. The peripteral temple itself presents six columns along its facade and ten along its length in Corinthian style but with unfluted shafts.

In the *impluvium* of the house of Dionysos at Dougga, a third-century mosaic was discovered in which Ulysses is depicted tied to the mast of his ship in order to resist the song of the Sirens. The town also has a fine theater whose second-century *cavea* could accommodate 3500 spectators. The colonnade and the stage wall have been skillfully restored with the help of fragments found on site.

The city of Sbeïtla (Sufetula), built at the beginning of the second century A.D. on flat terrain much further south, presents a regular ground plan with large orthogonal *insulae*, at the center of which is situated the forum with its three capitoline temples. The central one was dedicated to Jupiter, with those on either side dedicated to Juno and Minerva. A triple arch, built in 139 during the reign of Antoninus Pius, forms the entrance, slightly off the central axis, to the temples. This triad of sanctuaries, side by side on a single podium, constitutes an unusual group. The high podium, reached by stairways from the lateral temples, contains crypts. The three facades, a composite order in the center and Corinthian

Third century mosaic
At Bulla Regia (Tunisia) this fine third-century mosaic representing Venus, in the house known as the house of Amphitrite, decorates the living quarters created underground in order to escape summer heat.

Underground peristyle at Bulla Regia
For the summer, wealthy Romans duplicated their living quarters underground in order to enjoy a cool environment. The House of the Hunt possesses such an underground *atrium corinthicum*.

Page 195
Capitol of Dougga

The lofty tetrastyle facade of the Capitol of Dougga (Thugga) of A.D. 166 is dedicated to the triad of Jupiter, Juno, and Minerva. The Corinthian style of the porticus is very pure. On the tympanum features the apotheosis of Antoninus Pius, whom an eagle is carrying toward heaven.

Fourth century mosaic

Eternal theme of the exemplary hero, Ulysses is tied to the mast of his ship in order not to succumb to the song of the Sirens. Floor mosaic from Dougga dating from the fourth century.
(Musée National du Bardo, Tunis)

Temple of Juno Caelestis

The semicircular *peribolos* of the temple of Juno Caelestis at Dougga, with its porticus surrounding the podium that bears the Corinthian hexastyle sanctuary built between 222 and 235, under Severus Alexander.

on either side, overlook a huge courtyard lined with porticuses. On either side of the main sanctuary, vaulted passages lead back to the apses of the buildings that form an almost intact rear facade.

In ancient Thysdrus (modern El Djem) in the eastern part of the country at the edge of the Sahel desert, between Sousse and Sfax, the enormous silhouette of an amphitheater towers over the modern town. Almost as vast as the Colosseum of Rome, this ceremonial building of the second and third centuries A.D. measures some 150 meters in length with a height of 36 meters. It could accommodate 30,000 spectators. The construction of this colossal building is evidence of the size of the revenue generated by the products of the olive groves of the area that, in addition to their culinary purposes, also served in the process of soap-making, cosmetics, and dye.

Page 196 top
The temples of Sbeitla
The three temples of Sbeitla, haughty remains of ancient Sufetula, a town in the south of Tunisia, form a complex dedicated to the capitoline triad. On a single podium housing impressive crypts, the three sanctuaries of Hadrianic date (second century) are tetrastyles in a composite order (the temple of Jupiter in the center) and Corinthian (the temples of Juno and Minerva).

Page 196 bottom
Symbol of the triad
The apse of the capitoline temples of Sbeitla, with the three juxtaposed buildings between which vaulted corridors allow the movement of people, forms one of the most complete sacred complexes of Roman Africa. Note that the temple of Jupiter is pseudoperipteral (embedded columns) while the sanctuaries of Juno and Minerva have pilasters around the *cella* that barely stand out.

Top
Access for Spectators
The arcades of the amphitheater of El Djem were created, as was the whole building, out of large blocks of porous tufa, which did not permit the construction of wide bays or ample passageways.

The amphitheater of El Djem
With its three stories of arcades punctuated by embedded columns, the amphitheater of El Djem (ancient Thysdrus), in the south of Tunisia, is one of the largest of the empire, measuring 150 by 124 meters. It was built in the third century, and the upheavals of the great crisis left it unfinished.

Mosaics

North Africa has contributed a considerable number of mosaic pavements to the archaeology of antiquity. To a greater extent than in Pompeii and Herculaneum, where this art was already present, this form of floor decoration developed particularly in Tunisia during the second and third centuries A.D. in the villas of the rich landowners. The technique used by the local artists to decorate the opulent homes consisted of assembling small cubes (or *tessera*) of marble, colored stone, or glass to create geometric or figurative compositions. These elements, after careful arrangement, were fixed in a bed of mortar. The large designs, initially executed in black on a white background, soon became multicuslored, occasionally in very bright colors. Certain mosaics consisted of a central medallion motif (an *emblema*) usually executed in a realistic and finely worked style. Around this central motif, various borders in floral or rythmic designs were depicted.

According to Pliny the Elder, "The pavements owed their origins to Greece," a term that includes Asia Minor, since the author stresses "the fame that Sosus of Pergamon acquired." He adds that "the first pavement made of 'lozenges' [in Rome] was executed in the temple of Jupiter Capitoline, after the beginning of the Third Punic War" (149 B.C.). Since Greek antiquity, figurative mosaics with multiple borders have depicted scenes that were akin to those shown on floor carpets. The archaeological discovery in 1949 of the famous Pazyryk carpet in Siberia, dating back to 500 B.C., confirms this analogy. Probably made by a Persian tribe for a Scythian chieftain, this large knotted carpet (200 by 183 centimeters) displays Graeco-Lydian and Achemenidian influences, recognizable from the motifs of the borders: stars, rose shapes, crosses, gryphons, and winged lions, to which friezes of horses and deer are added. The art of Middle Eastern carpet mak-

Roman mosaic

Roman mosaic from ancient Hadrumetus (Sousse), illustrating the four seasons: here, summer, with its fruit and harvest. In the center of a rich leafy garland, the head and shoulders figure forms an *emblema*, which is made of small fragments of mosaic. (Musée archéologique, Sousse)

ing seems to have inspired the decoration of floor mosaics where the decorative repertoire is often similar. In a sense, a mosaic is a carpet made of stone, with its animal or floral motifs, not to mention its meanders, its fretwork, and its Greek patterns. In the Roman provinces of Africa, stylistic evolution produced a freer, more figurative style, stemming from a popular tradition. The themes dealt with religious mythology, circus games, and scenes from daily life in a series of spontaneous creations that differ from Pompeian works. The mosaic art of the luxurious villas built in North Africa by major landowners is a veritable architectural pattern book: palaces, porticoes, castles, hippodromes, mausoleums, cabins, and other objects can all be seen there. There are boats and seafaring ships, lions, tigers, bears, elephants, deer, fish, shellfish, and shells. Human figures are also represented. The gods take on the appearance of lords and ladies; dancers rub shoulders with Hercules; Ulysses with Dionysos and his retinue; Neptune on his chariot gallops over the ocean; naked naiads, wearing only jewels, swim among the dolphins. The artists did not forget to include horse racing and chariot races with audiences of gamblers. Scenes of circus games, where the gladiator is face to face with panthers or wolves, are placed next to peaceful harvest scenes. Diners reclining on their couches, served by young servants in the *triclinium*, alternate with fishermen in their boats. There is no need for scholarly interpretation of these mosaics. Any symbolic or emblematic meaning is immediately evident: the four seasons, legend of Venus, Bacchus and his retinue, and so forth. For the rest, the art evokes the joyful existence of a "golden present" and an ambience of carefree well-being and contentment. Here, the dividends of the *pax Romana* are depicted. One of the chief merits of these floor mosaics, outward signs of happiness, is to introduce us to the intimate lives of wealthy traders and rich landowners, evidence of the prosperity of an imperial age dispensing the philosophy of *carpe diem* through everyday enchantments.

The triumph of Bacchus
The *thiasus* or procession of Dionysos or Bacchus, god of wine, advances beneath the climbing vine. The god holding the thyrsus drives his ceremonial chariot drawn by four tigers. Preceded by a dancing nymph playing the tambourine, he is accompanied by a winged figure of Victory. (Musée archéologique, Sousse)

This prosperity did not entail an abandonment to material enjoyments alone. Roman Africa had its share of intellectuals, philosophers, and poets. Among the great names deserving mention are Apulius of Madauros (125–170), author of the *Golden Ass*, a picaresque story full of imagination; the rhetor Marcus Cornelius Fronton of Cirta (100–175), friend of Antoninus and tutor of Marcus Aurelius; and the jurist Tertullian of Carthage (155–222), a convert who became one of the first Christian writers in the Latin tongue.

The Great Cities of Tripolitania

In modern Libya, the western province – Tripolitania, as it was known – owes its name to the three main towns that flourished there: Sabratha, Oea (present-day Tripoli), and Leptis Magna. The first and last of these are the most interesting from an archaeological point of view since they were never later reoccupied. Founded in the Punic period, these towns enjoyed a meteoric rise during the imperial age, culminating when Septimius Severus showered his native land with the benefits that flowed from the imperial throne.

The main resource of the region was trade, together with some agriculture. It was linked to black Africa by the caravan trails that ran from the Mediterranean to Gao on the loop of the Niger, across the Fezzan and Tibesti regions. The trade was mainly in ivory, gold, feathers and ostrich eggs, wild beasts earmarked for the imperial circuses, and black slaves, in ever-increasing numbers.

There is little evidence of the contacts established by the trans-saharan routes mentioned by Pliny on the subject of ancient Garama. Sir Mortimer Wheeler makes special mention of the mausoleum of Djerma, the southernmost Roman monument in Africa. Situated deep in the Fezzan region, it looked like a small temple with an Ionic porticus. These meager ruins nevertheless demonstrate that relations existed relatively early. The proconsul Cornelius Balbus had led an expedition in 19 B.C. against the Garamantes. In A.D. 69, Valerius Festus invaded the Fezzan region on another punitive expedition, following an uprising by nomadic tribes. Such "pacification" operations enabled stable commercial links to be established.

Overlooking the sea, the town of Sabratha is made up of several districts. The oldest part, surrounded by walls, was built against a range of rocks that formed a natural harbor. In the time of Antoninus Pius, a new town was built farther east on

Right

Longitudinal section of the theater of Sabratha

Its high stage wall was protected by a roof projecting to the edge of the *orchestra*. In order to support the seating of the *cavea*, there are three stories of semicircular arcades. Vaulted passageways enabled spectators to reach their seats. At the top, an arcaded ambulatory completes the whole.

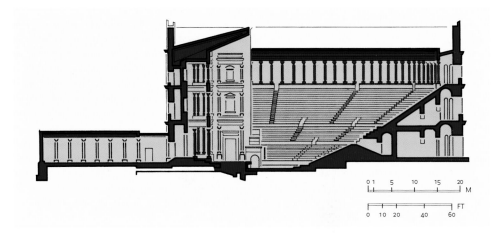

Top

The architecture of ancient drama

The majority of Roman cities of Tripolitania were founded during the Phoenician period as maritime centers. At the edge of the sea are preserved ruins of Sabratha's theater (Libya), with the three stories of its *frons scaenae* behind the arcades of the *cavea* built on flat terrain.

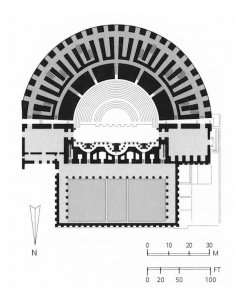

Classical theater design

The plan of the theater of Sabratha reveals a perfect hemicycle, with a deep stage whose colonnaded arrangement is punctuated by three *exedras*. On either side stand two large blocks intended to house stage machinery, dressing rooms, and props. Behind the stage wall, a quadriporticus takes up the theme introduced by the theater of Pompey in Rome.

A setting for the apparition of rulers or gods

Two of the three stories of the *frons scaenae* of the theater of Sabratha. Its central and lateral superposed canopies occupy the *exedras* that punctuate the facade. Below, the mixtilinear *pulpitum* displays alcoves and projections that are alternately semicircular and rectangular. Although the building was built in the Antonine period, the stage wall bears the hallmark of Severus, whose munificence rained down on the whole of North Africa.

a rectilinear town plan. In A.D. 180, a large theater was built in the center. When the site was abandoned, most of the masonry remained, enabling various Italian teams to carry out a meticulous restoration program between 1927 and 1937. The theater's *cavea* is 92 meters in diameter and is supported by 29 arches on three levels, with seven flights of stairs to reach the seats. This is an essentially Roman building in character; instead of being built into the flank of a hill, it rises freestanding on level ground.

Archaeologists most notably reconstructed the extraordinary stage building of the theater with its three stories of columns, the whole measuring 25 meters high and 40 meters wide. This grandiose *frons scaenae*, enlivened by projecting and recessed structures, is decorated with canopies set into semicircular recesses. It overlooks a *pulpitum* whose niches, alternately rounded and square, are decorated with relief sculptures depicting scenes from tragedy and mime.

On the subject of this sumptuous facade, which reflected the architectural ideal that Pompeian painting had prefigured, Gilbert Picard writes that "at Sabratha the wealth of columns decorating the upper balconies or creating airy pavilions, through which the sky and the sea of the Syrtes could be seen, truly recreated the enchanted palace where Eros received Psyche."

The canopy confers a divine rank on the personalities or statues that it shelters. Thus the celestial palace, represented by the *frons scaenae*, is peopled with gods and goddesses, and symbolizes a marvelous afterlife. The openings in the stage wall reflect an image of urban geography (the door of the palace in the center, flanked by the doors of the town and the port), or of social hierarchy (the royal door in the center), or of celestial hierarchy (the gods often appeared on the upper levels). Moreover, in order to visualize the appearance of the theatrical scenes, one must imagine how the role of the decor intervened with its statues peopling the upper levels, its polychromy and omnipresent gold. Like the gods, rulers appeared before the spectators, particularly during deification ceremonies, to which the sumptuous setting of the *frons scaenae* lent an extraordinary brilliance.

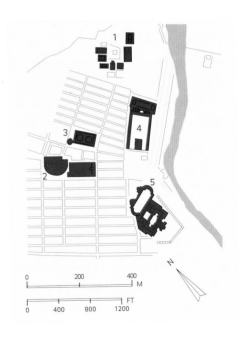

The port city of Leptis Magna
On the banks of the Wadi Lebda, the port city of Leptis Magna (Libya):
1. The Old Forum
2. Theater
3. Market (*macellum*)
4. New Forum
5. Baths of Hadrian

Plan of the Old Forum of Leptis Magna

Built for the most part by Calpurnius Pison, proconsul of Africa around 5 B.C.:

1. Temple of Rome and Augustus
2. Porticus
3. Byzantine church
4. Basilica
5. Curia

Architectural pomp

Dating from the Severan period (after 193) the New Forum of Leptis Magna possesses a homogeneous design:

1. Square surrounded by porticuses
2. Temple of the *gens Septima*, dedicated to the worship of the dynasty of Septimius Severus
3. Transversal basilica with three naves and two apses in the form of *exedras*.

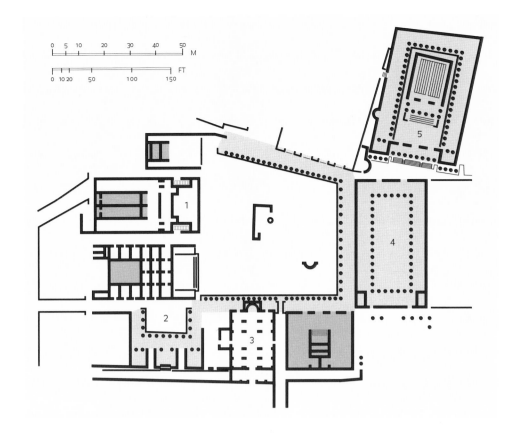

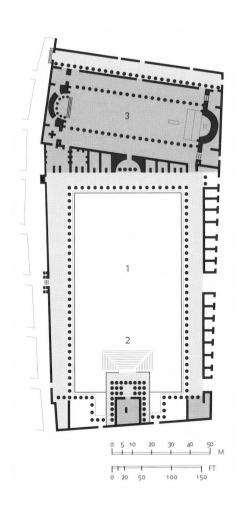

The Splendor of Leptis Magna

The easternmost city of Latin-speaking proconsular Africa is Leptis Magna, the home of Septimius Severus (farther east lies Cyrene, where the Greek language was entrenched for centuries). The port town, which dates back to Punic colonizers, was developed in Roman times shortly before the beginning of the modern era with Caesar's annexation of the town in 46 B.C. The first forum (the Old Forum or *forum vetus*) occupied a sliver of land between the sea and the course of the Wadi Lebdah, whose estuary formed a safe haven for trading ships.

This Old Forum, consisting of a series of sanctuaries, including a Temple of Rome and Augustus, a curia and a basilica, was the work of the proconsul Calpurnius Pison between 5 and 2 B.C. Farther to the southwest, the town had already acquired, between 9 and 8 B.C., a theater (Augustan period) and a superb market, formed by a quadriporticus, 73 by 43 meters, surrounding two circular pavilions. This *macellum* built by Annobal Rufus, whose name indicates Phoenician and Roman ancestry, was restored several times. In 126, during Hadrian's reign, sumptuous baths were built outside the cadastered grid of streets. They contained a sanctuary dedicated to Hercules, patron of the city. Behind the baths, a fine curvilinear nymphaeum stood on a triangular area.

During the Severan period (after 193), a lighthouse and an inner harbor were built, like that of Trajan at Ostia, as well as an ostentatious assembly of monuments and a colonnaded triumphal avenue, 20 meters wide, following the course of the Wadi and adjoining the New Forum. Covering a surface of 200 by 100 meters, the New Forum combined a civic basilica with a vast square surrounded by a porticus. Over the columns of the porticus were arcades whose spandrels bore the heads of Atargatis-Scylla in sculpted relief, like the *umbo* of a shield.

At one end of this square stood the Temple of the *gens Septima*, a centrally placed octostyle building dominating the surroundings. A narrowing flight of steps led up to the high podium (5.8 meters). This dynastic imperial temple contained 32 monolithic shafts of Aswan granite.

At the other end of the square, 60 meters wide, an *exedra* in the role of a monu-

mental gateway led to a vast transversal basilica built between 210 and 216. The arrangement of a square adjoining a transversal building recalls the Forum of Trajan in Rome. Situated on either side of this *exedra* with its screen of columns were various chambers. These were slightly more shallow on the eastern side than on the western side, effectively disguising a slight nonalignment between the square and the basilica.

A reference to the Basilica Ulpia at this juncture is not misplaced: The Severan building had dimensions that almost equaled those of its precursor. This hall, 90 by 40 meters, with three naves divided by two stories of columns with lateral galleries, featured apses at both ends and was covered by a wooden coffered ceiling. In both scale and rectangular basilical format, the two creations, though separated by a century, demonstrate many similarities.

A profound stylistic evolution
The arcades of the porticus surrounding the Severan forum at Leptis Magna, reconstituted here without the columns' shafts. The "baroquization" of the forms is underlined by the recourse to arches at the top of the columns, instead of architraves.

The Theater of Leptis Magna

Built in A.D. 1–2, the theater of Leptis Magna is, surprisingly, one of the first buildings of its kind in the Roman world after Pompey's theater in Rome. However, its *cavea* conforms to the Greek model; it is cut into the rock of a hill instead of resting on supporting arcades arranged in a semicircle. As if to underline its similarity with Pompey's creation, the complex features a central rectangular hexastyle sanctuary or *sacellum* at the top of the *cavea*. This small temple was dedicated initially to Ceres, with a subsequent association with Augustus, who was worshipped from Tiberius's time. Here again, the theater is linked with the worship of sovereigns, as was seen at Praeneste and Tivoli. Another African example of this phenomenon is the theater of Guelma (formerly Calama) in Algeria, where a small, vaulted hall with a half-dome apse overlooks the seating.

The theater of Leptis Magna, built just after the death of Vitruvius, applies the acoustic imperatives that the theoretician had stressed in Book V of his *Ten Books of Architecture* regarding the circular projection of the voice, as Aristotle had codified it. This justified the curve of the seating. In studying diagrams of the standard designs of Greek and Roman theaters, Pierre Gros points out a curious comparison made by Vitruvius: "The circumference is to be drawn; and in it four equilateral triangles are to be described touching the circumference at intervals (just as with the twelve celestial signs, astronomers calculate from the musical division of the constellations)." In this extract, the author of the *Ten Books of Architecture* refers to astrology, and in particular to "the configurations suggested by Geminos of Rhodes, probably contemporary with Vitruvius" (Pierre Gros), in the way that his predecessor, Varro, implicitly did in his aviary in evoking the stars Lucifer and Vesper that revolved there.

At Leptis Magna, the similarity to the theater of Pompey continues with the quadriporticus *post-scaenam*, built behind the stage building. It is true that the colonnade is smaller here and has a trapezoidal shape, but it nevertheless occupies the same position. Moreover, in the center, on the same axis as the theater, stands the temple of the *dei Augusti*, built in A.D. 43, again underlining the close association between sanctuary and stage.

The theater of Leptis Magna, 88 meters in diameter, acquired its stage wall only in the second century A.D. (it is partially restored today.) As at Sabratha, the columns stand out against a marine horizon. The main interest of the building, apart from its state of preservation, lies in the many sculptures that still decorate the *cavea*. They confer a picturesque liveliness to this theater, displaying evidence of the statuary decor that existed everywhere during antiquity.

The importance, the opulence and the prominent position of these theaters are surprising. What purpose did they serve? True, the classics (Graeco-Roman tragedies and comedies) were still performed. But more often than not, extracts and anthologies were performed that served to show the actors at their best advantage. The works of Plautus, translations of Menander and other Hellenistic authors, farces, mimes, and ballets were all performed here. Satirical plays were performed on stage, as were plays for special occasions. Poetry was also recited. Moreover, the *cavea* was used as the venue for "magical" shows featuring scantily clad dancers and also for variety shows.

But the theaters were soon pressed into service for meetings of a political nature. The civic population was summoned to the *cavea*, and popular assemblies or *ecclesia* involving all the citizens were held there. The *evergetes* were proclaimed, and the opinion of the plebians was consulted there. In the presence of the emperor or his local representative, who sat in a central box called the *tribunalia*, a liturgy of participation was practised, derived from imperial religion. The authorities carried out the law and justice there, announced new laws, and pronounced verdicts *ex cathedra*.

Plan of the theater at Leptis Magna

The theater at Leptis Magna dates from A.D. 1–2. The semicircular *cavea* opens up facing the sea. Behind the stage wall, the trapezoidal quadriporticus surrounds a small sanctuary dedicated to imperial worship.

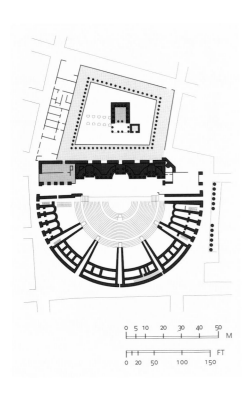

```
0  5 10   20   30   40   50
|__|_|____|____|____|____|  M

|___|___|_____|_____|  FT
0  20  50    100   150
```

The people's assembly (ecclesia)
The theater of Leptis Magna, built under Augustus, was enlarged and given a new stage wall under Septimius Severus. Its vast *cavea*, set against the hill, with its entrances (*vomitoria*) intact, constitutes a magnificent hemicycle facing the Mediterranean.

In this way, the *cavea* represented the body of society arranged in a hierarchical order on the seats, where official positions became increasingly hereditary during the late empire. This use of theaters should not be underestimated. It allows us to understand why these buildings were maintained and enlarged until the end of antiquity. Their function was no longer limited to the literary concerns of a population. The nature of the performances had changed since these monuments typical of the Graeco-Roman world were built.

Spared the great invasions that swept over the West in the middle of the third century, Roman Africa continued to lead a placid existence until the incursions of the Vandals in 429. It was only finally lost with the installation of Genseric at Carthage in 447.

Page 209
Statuary of the *frons scaenae*
The statuary decorating the *frons scaenae* of the theater of Leptis Magna stands in front of columns, carefully restored to return to this building all its original beauty under the Tripolitanian sun.

The Grandiose Creations
of the Late Empire

Baths, Basilicas and Fortifications

Page 211
Bust of the Emperor Caracalla
The son of Septimius Severus and of the Syrian Julia Domna, who reigned from 211 to 217, had given to all the free inhabitants of the Empire the right to live in a Roman city. His reign marked the start of the unsettled period that led to the great crisis of the third century. (Museo Capitolino, Rome)

Fashion: A constant cycle
Dressed in a very modern "bikini," this gymnast adorns a mosaic of the Villa Romana del Casale at Piazza Armerina (Sicily), believed to be the home to which one of the Tetrarchs retired. Maximian Hercules probably built it to live there after his abdication in 305. The technical quality of the mosaic bears many similarities to those in the Roman villas of Tunisia.

The Roman Empire was shaken by serious crisis in the middle of the third century A.D.; the military order broke down (235–270), and there were waves of Germanic and Sassanid invasions (251–278). The effect was so far-reaching that Rome's social, political, and economic order seemed mortally wounded. But by sheer will, Rome achieved an extraordinary recovery through Aurelius (270-275) and in Diocletian's establishment of the tetrarchy.

As H.P. L'Orange has pointed out, the arrival of Diocletian led to a complete reshaping not only of the institutions but of the whole structure of Roman society. The hereditary character of public positions, the obligation to work for the state, and the military style of administration went hand in hand with the establishment of a new system of power and a territorial subdivision of tasks that foreshadowed the division between the western and eastern empire. These measures were an attempt to stabilize power threatened by military uprisings and the secession of provinces proclaimed by upstart emperors upheld by the rabble. Diocletian decreed that he would share his authority with another Augustine and would at the same time nominate two Caesars. The two Augustines would reign for 20 years, then would abdicate in favor of the Caesars, who would replace them.

In practice, Diocletian and Maximian reigned in the image of Jupiter and Hercules, with whom they identified. Galerius and Constantius Chlorus assisted them. Consequently the empire acquired four capital cities: Nicomedia and Milan for the Augustines and Sirmium and Trier for the Caesars. Thus Rome lost its imperial role.

This scheme fell victim to personal ambitions, however, and worked only until the abdication of Diocletian in 305. This profound transformation of the regime can be described as the principate giving way to a "dominate" where the influence of the state played an increasingly important role in the daily lives of citizens. Consequently, structural reform was accompanied by autocratic assertion necessary to restore the power of the ruler. As a result, imperial deification, and the court rituals that accompanied it, became more accentuated. Meanwhile, the cohesiveness of the population became crucial for consolidating authority, which explains why the major architectural enterprises of the period aimed to bring luxury and well-being to everyone.

Major Projects

The restoration of order could have been limited to regaining the initiative, containing the threat, and reinforcing central power. But the measures taken were also characterized, on the artistic level, by an extraordinary momentum, a new desire of affirmation, and a spirit that expressed itself in grandeur and magnificence. It was especially in the field of huge public and utilitarian creations that this period asserted itself, preceding the conversion of the empire to Christianity and the foundation by Constantine in 330 of a new capital named Constantinople, on the site of ancient Byzantium.

During Aurelius's reign, a strong city wall was built in brick, restricting the city

of Rome to a confined area. Its circumference was approximately 19 kilometers, with 18 gates and 381 towers. This project was a considerable enterprise. A series of monuments was destroyed and their materials incorporated into the defensive fortifications.

The building of city walls was also undertaken in many other cities threatened by the Germanic invaders, in particular, the towns situated on the frontier of the Rhine, such as Trier and Cologne. Combining structural power and the techniques of siegecraft, the Porta Nigra of Trier is a good example of efficient design, with its semicircular towers projecting forward in order to facilitate defensive fire on assailants. But this gate was also imbued with symbolic meaning. Its heavy outline, its engaged colonnettes, its barely sculpted capitals: everything in its design expressed strength, ruggedness, stability, and imperial authority.

After a ruthless military crackdown that showed the Romans' determination to survive, the reestablishment of power allowed them to display once more the spirit of generosity and splendor that had characterized the glory of the Severan dynasty. With the exception of works connected with fortifications of the *limes* and of towns, the purpose of the last sovereigns of the Roman Empire in the West was concentrated on the construction of public baths and basilicas.

In order to gain the support of the citizens, those in power took into consideration the wishes of the masses, endowing them with public places whose beauty was comparable to the state rooms of the imperial palace.

The institution of public baths derives from a Roman tradition dating back to the end of the Republic and the early days of the Empire. There were already interesting examples of the phenomenon at Pompeii and Herculaneum. However, from Nero and Titus onward, baths were conceived on a much larger scale and acquired

Part of the walls of Aurelian, intended to protect Rome
With its projecting towers whose base slopes outward to consolidate the structure, this fortification measuring 19 kilometers – and which includes a considerable number of other uses – was restored many times during the medieval period. At the top of the towers were platforms permitting the positioning of war machines (*balistas*).

Page 215
The Porta Appia
Part of Aurelian's fortifications (270–275), the Porta Appia (*Porta San Sebastiano*), in the south of Rome, is the result of a series of modifications. To the two original towers, the square substructures of marble were added in the time of Honorius (early fifth century). The upper part of the semicircular towers was also raised later.

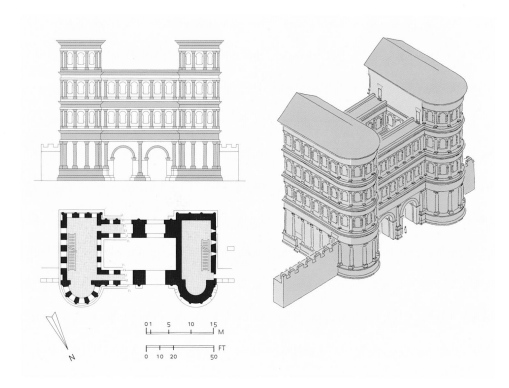

Elevation, plan, and axonometric drawing of the Porta Nigra
The town of Trier (Germany), ancient Augusta Treverorum, became the imperial capital under the Tetrarchy and housed the Emperor Constantius Chlorus from 293.

Rome expresses its defensive outlook
The Porta Nigra at Trier is the classic example of defensive architecture of the end of the third century, with its semicircular projecting towers and stories of bays punctuated by embedded columns. It was built in large stone blocks. The apse, in the left part of the picture, is a medieval addition, from the time when the building was used as a church.

The Aula Palatina in Trier
The Basilica of Trier is a vast Aula Palatina 70 meters long and 27 meters wide, entirely built in brick. The superposed windows, set back, cause the projecting buttresses to animate the facade. The architectural language of the late Empire abandoned the use of columns and pilasters in favor of the exalted grandeur of a very spare, unified architectural style.

A formula that the Christians were to perpetuate
Interior view of the Aula Palatina of Trier, with its reconstructed ceiling. The roof was now made of wood with coffering and stood around 30 meters from the ground. In Constantine's time (310), architecture abandoned solid vaulting and adopted a lighter system, which would prevail in Constantinian basilicas, after the conversion of the emperor to Christianity.

their characteristic appearance. These opulent constructions intended for large numbers of people adopted a symmetrical structure, duplicating several amenities (*palaestra,* garden, changing rooms, etc.) on either side of the central axis that structured the three halls of the main baths – hot (*caldarium*), warm (*tepidarium*), and cold (*frigidarium*)– soon augmented by an open-air swimming pool (*natatio*).

The Roman baths combined enclosed spaces, intended for the activity of bathing itself, with "sporting" amenities in the fashion of Greek gymnasia. These were situated in open-air courtyards surrounded by quadriporticuses and in gardens with walls that isolated the complex from the town.

As early as the Baths of Trajan in A.D. 104, the size of such a complex was considerable: 310 by 225 meters. The outer precinct that was made up of five huge exedras (the main one was 120 meters wide) contained in turn a complex 190 by 165 meters. Its center was a cruciform *frigidarium* 60 meters long. The sides of the square pool were 50 meters in length.

The characteristic layout of Roman baths was thus definitively established with only minor variations in later buildings. But with the Baths of Caracalla, built around 216, a substantial enlargement of these thermal installations occurred. The surrounding wall, with its two large lateral *exedras,* was a rectangle 410 meters wide by 380 meters deep, an area of 15 hectares. And the buildings stretched over a width of 210 meters, including a sumptuous circular *caldarium*, 55 meters in diameter. This domed rotunda stood in front of a *tepidarium*, which in turn overlooked the huge hall of the *frigidarium*, covered by a series of three groined vaults 65 meters long and 29 meters wide (almost 2000 square meters).

Late Roman mosaic
Decorative mosaic tiling covering the floor of one of the halls in the Baths of Caracalla in Rome. In Roman baths, the use of mosaic even extended to the vaults, foreshadowing the use that Byzantium was to make of it.

General plan of the Baths of
Caracalla in Rome

1. Peripheral gardens inside the
   boundary wall
2. *Natatio* or large pool
3. Basilical hall
4. Behind the *tepidarium*, the
   large rotunda of the *caldarium*
5. Palaestras flanked by *exedras*
6. *Exedras* with apsidal rooms

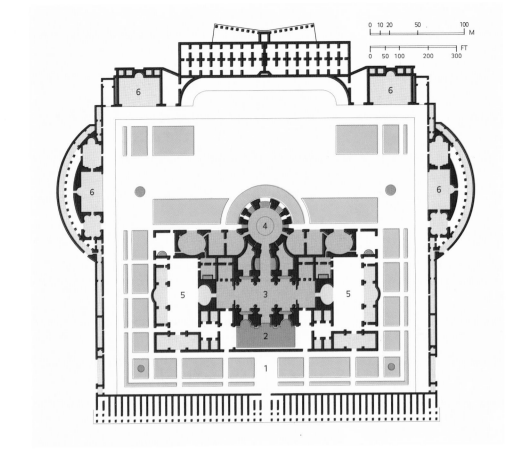

Page 218

**Large arcade in concrete masonry
in the Baths of Caracalla in Rome**
These baths were begun in 212
and opened to the public in A.D.
216. The basilical hall with groined
vault to which these arches give
access is 58 by 24 metres. The
whole symmetrical layout is duplicated to offer the same facilities
to men and to women.

In these opulent constructions, the care of the physical body (baths, swimming, steam baths, massage, running, gymnastic exercises) was not the only service offered to visitors. They could attend debates, declamations, and musical concerts. In addition there was a library. The decor included masterpieces, in painting and sculpture, forming a gallery and museum. In effect, these establishments combined sport and culture in one center.

During the rule of the Tetrarchs, the luxury and splendor became even more accentuated. The Baths of Diocletian in Rome cover an area of 390 by 370 meters, and the buildings alone reach 235 by 150 meters, amounting to approximately 30,000 square meters of roofing. The central cruciform *frigidarium*, whose original appearance can be imagined, transformed by Michelangelo into the Church of Santa Maria degli Angeli, measures 66 by 48 meters (28 meters for the nave alone). It was also covered by three groined vaults whose elegance can be admired, above the powerful embedded columns that decorate the interior. The circular *tepidarium* (20 meters in diameter) surmounted by a fine cupola with a small *oculus*, now forms the vestibule leading to the church.

In his capital of Trier, Constantius Chlorus (305–311) built baths on a similar model. The spread of these thermal establishments throughout the empire was intended, like *panem et circences* (bread and games), to reinforce the political and social cohesion of the Roman world. From the Severan period, baths proliferated in all towns of any importance. The originality of the baths at Trier consists in the use of a semicircular design for the majority of the pools surrounded by apses. In the architecture of this rigorously symmetrical complex with its circular domed halls, curvilinear forms proliferated. Here, the *frigidarium*, covered with the usual groined vaults, reached a length of 58 meters and a width of 22 meters.

The decision to resort to solid vaulting, instead of coffered wooden ceilings, was a necessity because of the humidity in the buildings. Concrete or brick also provided better insulation.

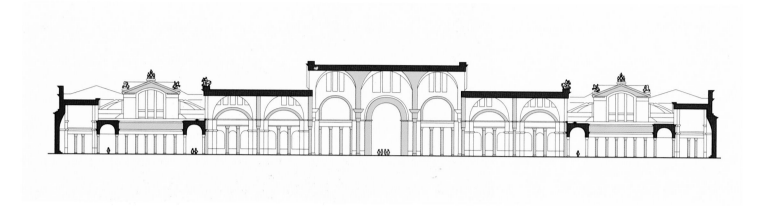

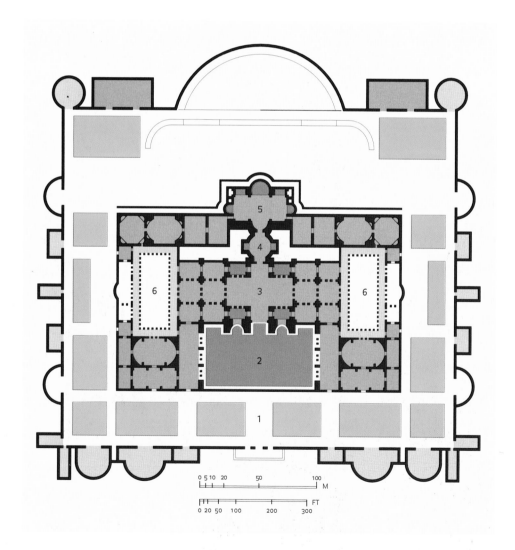

Top

An extraordinary architectural complex

Cross section of the central core of the Baths of Diocletian in Rome, built between 298 and 306. Symmetrically designed, the principal group consists on each side of open-air *palaestrae* surrounded by porticoes, then, on either side of the basilical hall, of two-bay lateral halls. The three central bays reach a height of 30 meters, forming a huge hall under a cross vault.

General plan of the Baths of Diocletian in Rome

1. Entrance to the gardens
2. *Natatio*
3. Basilical hall
4. Rotunda of the *tepidarium*
5. *Caldarium*
6. *Palaestrae*

On either side of the large central exedra, rotundas were built at the corners of the edifice.

Vestibule of the Church of Santa Maria degli Angeli
With its vault and *oculus* and seven rows of coffers, the hall of the *tepidarium*, whose space is reminiscent of the Pantheon, today acts as the vestibule of the Church of Santa Maria degli Angeli, converted by Michelangelo in the basilical hall of the Baths of Diocletian in Rome.

This section on the central axis of the Baths of Diocletian shows the spatial organization, with the different halls in relation to one another.

Baths converted to a church
The strong and lofty cross vaults that survive intact in the Baths of Diocletian covered the basilical hall that Michelangelo and Vanvitelli transformed into the church of Santa Maria degli Angeli. The original nature of the hall was only slightly modified by its radically new function. Marble and granite columns, thermal windows, and polychrome marble veneers remained in place.

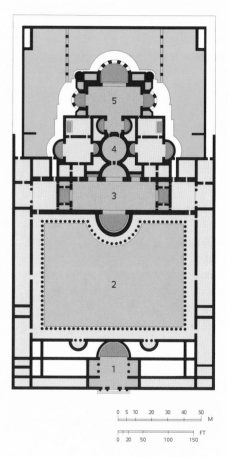

The end of the Roman Empire is often viewed as a period of decline; on the contrary, in architectural terms, it led to an unquestionable peak of achievement. This was demonstrated in the creation of internal space, the perfecting of the technology of concrete construction, and the luxury of installations intended for the general population who enjoyed not only the comfort of the baths, but also the beauty of the rich constructions, decorated with magnificent materials. A profusion of colored marble, breccia marble, porphyry, pink granite, alabaster, bronze, and other materials. decorated these baths, not to mention the splendid floor mosaics, and wall mosaics in glass with glittering reflections, introduced by the Tetrarchy in its utilitarian buildings, and soon to be seen decorating the apses of Byzantine churches. The "baroque" nature of the decoration of this functional architecture was echoed in the structure of the apses and curvilinear exedras.

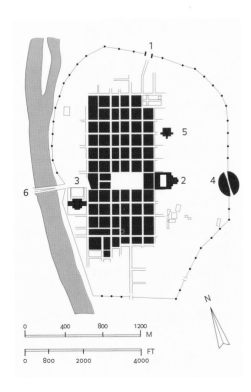

The Major Imperial Basilicas

In the late Empire, concrete was also used to roof certain major basilicas. In Rome, the basilica of Maxentius and Constantine, built at the eastern end of the Roman Forum between 306 and 312 by the son of Maximian Hercules, employed the same techniques (on an even grander scale) that had been perfected in the thermal establishments. The building consisted of an immense internal space of 4000 square meters. Supported on four pillars, the nave itself measured 80 by 25 meters, covered with three groined vaults at a height of 39 meters above the ground. Only the side aisles and three semicircular vaults perpendicular to the nave survive today.

In Trier, the second western capital of the empire, Constantine built a vast basilica, the Aula Palatina, in 310. The building, well preserved, measures 70 by 27 meters and is around 30 meters in height. The hall concluded in a huge hemicyclic apse. Gardens surrounded by porticoes were arranged on either side of this basilical *aula*, and a rectangular main building 68 by 12 meters, which has now disappeared, stood in front in the role of antechamber, or narthex.

This brick architecture, comprising two stories of large semicircular openings between which stood projecting buttresses, formed a purified mass by its sober power. It was the embodiment of the "dominate," such as L'Orange described it. But in contrast to the basilica of Maxentius and Constantine in Rome, this Constantinian throne room did not resort to the usual style of concrete roof. According to a formula that was then beginning to gain currency, as much in Trier as in the first Church of Saint Peter's in Rome and the Christian basilicas in the East, the architect chose to cover the immense space by means of a coffered ceiling supported by the beams of an ambitious wooden structure 27 meters wide. This technique was to evolve in the West up to the beginning of the Romanesque period.

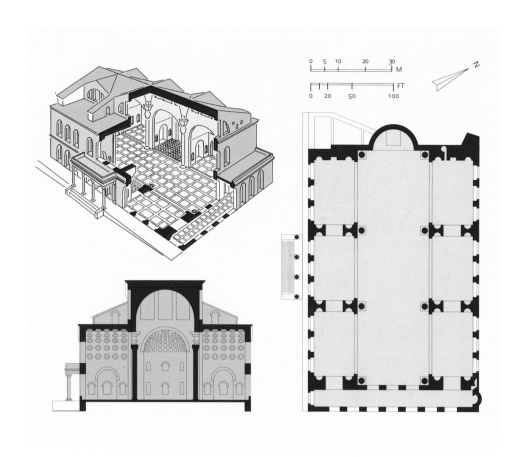

Open axonometric diagram, cross
section, and plan of the basilica
of Maxentius and Constantine
in Rome. The western apse contained a colossal statue of Constantine.

Villa Romana del Casale

Ultimate creation of Roman architecture proper, the Villa Romana del Casale at Piazza Armerina (Sicily) dating from the beginning of the fourth century, rejects both axial and symmetrical planning.

1. Entrance peristyle
2. Polygonal *atrium*
3. Vestibule
4. *Frigidarium*
5. *Natatio*
6. *Tepidarium* and *caldarium*
7. Peristyle vestibule
8. Large peristyle with nymphaeum
9. Promenade of the Great Hunt
10. Basilical *coenatio* with *exedra*
11. Small *coenatio* with *exedra*
12. Oval portico
13. *Aula* with three apses (*triconchos*)

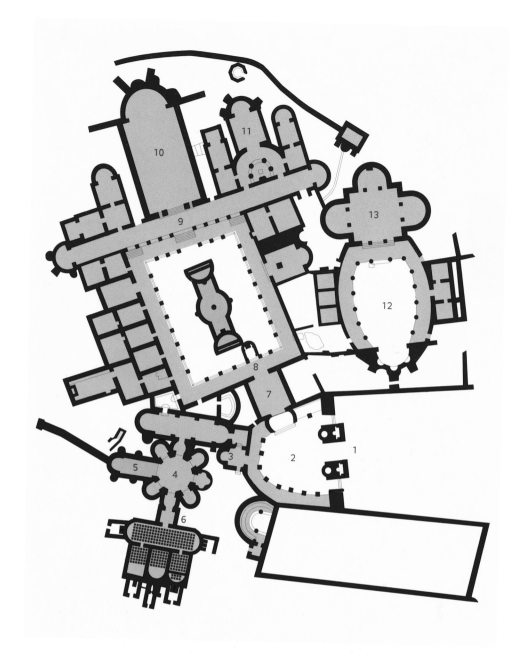

Page 224

Monumental Grandeur

In the Forum of Rome, the basilica of Maxentius and Constantine was one of the most grandiose architectural creations of late Empire. Covering an area 100 by 65 meters, this vast hall – of which only the three arches of the north side aisle survive – reached 35 meters high under the three cross vaults forming the main nave, which has disappeared. The large arcades of the side aisles were built of concrete with octagonal coffers, according to the technique characteristic of thermal buildings.

The Palace of a Tetrarch

The mention of the art of mosaic in the baths of the late Empire brings to mind the curious palace of Piazza Armerina, discovered in Sicily. Late in date, this large villa, in all probability built by Maximian Hercules (286–305) as a place to retire after his abdication, represents one of the most extraordinary groups of floor mosaics of all antiquity. It consists of almost 3500 square meters of figurative floor mosaics of exceptional quality, which in many respects are related to the mosaics in nearby Tunisia of the second and third centuries.

The ground plan of this complex was different in every respect from the rigorous orthogonal geometry of Diocletian's palace at Spalato on the Adriatic. Its free and organic character presents certain similarities to Hadrian's villa at Tivoli. Of course, by the nature of its dimensions and the compact appearance of its diverse, closely juxtaposed spatial units, the palatial organization of Piazza Armerina differs from Hadrian's pavilions scattered in the wilderness. But the scale, the imaginativeness, and the overall inspiration are similar.

In its own way, the Villa Romana del Casale at Piazza Armerina is a "folly" of sorts. But its labyrinth of rooms and corridors, its multifoil, trefoil, semicircular spaces, its basilical chambers, and its *exedras* are not so much the result of an

overflowing imagination as the consequence of a rigorous observance of punc-tilious court ritual, foreshadowing that of the Byzantine court. The palatial role of the complex is not called into question by the small scale of the rooms. On a surfa-ce area of 100 by 125 meters there are no fewer than 40 rooms, including the gar-den of the peristyle, thermal installations, the *atrium*, an entrance courtyard, and the portico.

The different areas seem to have grown almost anarchically, according to need, from the inside outward without symmetry or orthogonality. The building mater-ials are rustic, and the walls are built of irregular blocks covered in a thick coarse plaster. Only the Ionic columns elevate the tone of the materials. In effect, the main effort was concentrated in the mosaic flooring. But the originality of the buildings and the free way they interconnect never ceases to surprise.

Coming as it does at the end of the period of imperial architecture, Piazza Armerina constitutes a moving swan song. Such freshness and freedom, such unexpected discoveries demonstrate the prodigious resources that the pagan world still possessed on the eve of Christianity, that was to overturn not only the moral philosophy and the social structure of the old order but would impose new programs on architects, based on fundamentally different needs.

The Arch of Constantine in Rome
Located near the Colosseum, the Arch of Constantine commemor-ating the victory of the emperor at the Milvius Bridge in 312, was consecrated in 315. This three-bay arch "is an assemblage of sculp-tures and architectural fragments from various monuments" (F. Coarelli). The detail of a flying figure of Victory, carrying a trophy, situated over the main bay of the arch , is nevertheless characteristic of Constantinian sculpture by its barely accentuated relief.

CONCLUSION

The Evolution of the Interior Spaces

Fourth century silver platter
Detail of a fourth century silver plate from the hoard of late Empire tableware found at Augst (*Augusta Raurica*) in Switzerland. At the edge of a fish-rich sea where fishermen are busy, the depiction of symmetrically disposed buildings brings to mind the Palace of Diocletian at Spalato. (Römermuseum, Augst)

The overriding impression that emerges from this overview of four centuries of Roman architecture in the West is one of extraordinary prolixity. There were considerable variations in the types of building – their functions, plans, and forms. The architecture achieved spaces of extreme variety, complex spatial connections, and a remarkable relationship with the landscape. The wealth of concepts, the technology, the types of construction, the play between interior and exterior, where pure architecture met town-planning: all these elements contributed to the production of infinite wealth in technical solutions and in modes of expression.

Moreover, from Scotland to the Sahara and from the Atlantic to the Adriatic, there is indisputable unity, despite differences of climate, society, and environment. Behind the simple, decorative presence of the column, capital, and general outline (often derived from Greek models) there exists a broadly disseminated common language, based on the arch, the vault, and the dome. Thanks to them, Roman architecture is marked by a strong originality and specificity, placing it well above the modes of expression of earlier schools of architecture. Its novelty resides in the contribution of curvilinear elements achieved as much by sophisticated technological means as by the lightness of materials used (tufa, pumice stone, and brick).

Another striking feature is the wealth of typological formulas, the constant renewal of solutions. As part of a rigorous system derived from widespread centuriation, orthogonal town planning imposed itself where local conditions allowed. The Roman town was endowed with a repertoire of building types characteristic of Roman civilization: principally the forum, temple, capitol, palace, basilica, circus/stadium, theater, amphitheater, baths, and nymphaeum. To these principal components should be added the private dwelling situated in blocks (*insulae*), which adopted recurring designs according to the urban type. Outside the town, the home freely developed in innumerable variations of the country villa. Finally, in the purely ostentatious and commemorative domain, one should mention the honorific monuments (triumphal arch, trophy, tetrapyle, single column) and funerary memorials (tomb, mausoleum, cenotaph).

The importance of utilitarian buildings (*horrea* or warehouses, docks, factories, workshops, industrial installations) and the "links of the chain" that operated the infrastructure of the land (roads, bridges, aqueducts, dams, cisterns, ports) should also be noted.

In all domains, Roman architecture showed a remarkable stylistic coherence. The most important element in this architecture was the creation of ever larger internal spaces to respond to the requirements needed to satisfy an ever-increasing number of citizens and meet their expectations.

In Roman art, space was its prime ingredient. The essential element of creation consisted of space, rather than the play of light on solid mass. It was an art of the "cavity" or void. This took precedence over plastic elements, over the mass, and the external forms of a building.

The importance accorded to the interior resulted in a kind of inversion of the building inside out. The formula of the Greek temple, with its external colonnades and its tiny cella, culminates in Roman architecture in halls surrounded by columns on either side of the nave. This is demonstrated in sanctuaries, baths, halls playing the role of *aula regia*, and in certain basilicas.

But the interest of this architecture resides even more in the fact that it was charged with meaning; it transmitted a message and expressed itself through the intervention of a semiotic language that we must endeavor to understand. The buildings possessed an emblematic meaning, referring to a series of symbols, religious as well as political. It is these signs that can be analyzed by historians and by which the intention of the builders, although unspoken, can be grasped.

Such an approach allows us to understand the intentions that are expressed in building. Buildings that have been the object of many studies are invested with an ideological content that the specialist must decipher. Incursions into the most diverse domains, deification of sovereigns and imperial religion, religious dimension of the palace, aspiration to an afterlife depicted in the celestial cities of the *frons scaenae*, astronomy and astrology, allowing the placing of constructions in harmony with the universe, illuminate the underlying meaning expressed in architectural works and revealed by a careful examination of the philosophy of those who built them.

And even the utilitarian creations dedicated, in the case of the baths, to luxury and to well-being, finish by expressing the political and social motives of their creators. In all cases, they express the grandeur of a world that had made this quality one of the distinctive traits of its architecture, a grandeur that never limited itself to increasing, or even multiplying the dimensions of a work but tended to rethink the whole scheme on the basis of a new departure. This is the case of the Pantheon. Here we observe how the development, accompanied by an increase in scale, of an internal space of thermal structure and appearance, but with a religious function, albeit dynastic in character, led to a fundamental revolution in both formal and technological terms, in order to express more perfectly the idea of the universe over which the princeps reigned.

This same evolution is visible as much in the thermal halls as in the basilicas, where everything flows from the immensity of the internal space. These take such precedence over the exterior appearance that the latter almost seems sacrificed in favor of a more perfect spatial expression inside the building.

It is clear that the gigantism of Roman buildings was accompanied, as Sir Mortimer Wheeler put it, by a "transmutation" of the qualities of architecture. It flowed from a lucid awareness of the consequences that the immensity of the empire entailed and placed the notion of scale next to the very origins of architectural conception. The quest for grandeur was not only a challenge; it was the very embodiment of Roman civilization, as it had been with the pyramids of the Old Kingdom in Egypt. The one difference was that Rome replaced the idea of mass by the lightness of voids and ontological schematism by the dialectic of interior-exterior. The whole of Roman genius resides in this metamorphosis caused by the transition from mundane building blocks to the lyricism of inspired space.

Plan of the city of Rome
Overview of the main monuments
built in the imperial capital.

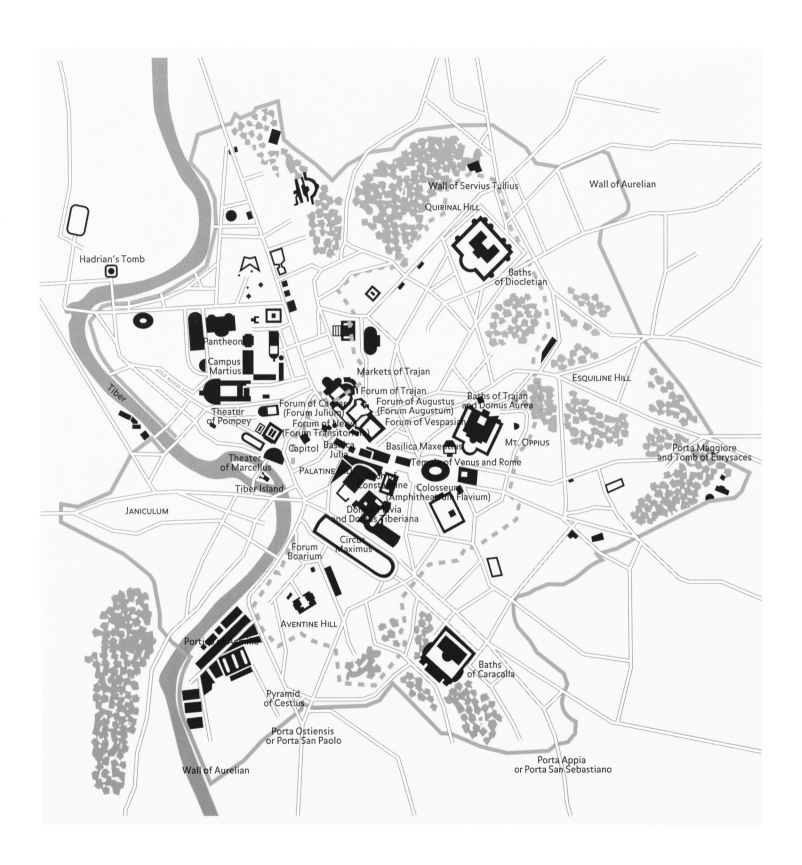

Wall of Servius Tullius

Wall of Aurelian

QUIRINAL HILL

Baths
of Diocletian

Hadrian's Tomb

ESQUILINE HILL

Markets of Trajan

Forum of Trajan

Pantheon

Forum of Augustus
(Forum Augustum)

Baths of Trajan
and Domus Aurea

Campus
Martius

Forum of Caesar
(Forum Julium)

Tiber

Forum of Nerva
(Forum Transitorium)

Forum of Vespasian

Theater
of Pompey

Porta Maggiore
and Tomb of Eurysaces

Mt. Oppius

Basilica
Julia

Basilica Maxentius

Capitol

Temple of Venus and Rome

Theater
of Marcellus

Arch of
Constantine

Colosseum
(Amphitheatrum Flavium)

PALATINE HILL

Tiber Island

Domus Flavia
and Domus Tiberiana

JANICULUM

Circus
Maximus

Forum
Boarium

AVENTINE HILL

Portico Aemilia

Baths
of Caracalla

Pyramid
of Cestius

Porta Ostiensis
or Porta San Paolo

Porta Appia
or Porta San Sebastiano

Wall of Aurelian

CHRONOLOGICAL TABLE

8th century	Villanovan huts
6th century	Cerveteri: Etruscan tombs
4th century	Alatri and Norba: city walls
273	Cosa: foundation and city walls
late 3rd century	Temple at Lago Argentina

Republican Temple of Fortuna Virilis
at the Forum Boarium in Rome

Terracotta model of a small Etruscan temple of
the third century B.C.

200–80	Pompeii: first style
179	Rome: Porticus Aemilia
c. 120	Rome: Forum Boarium, Temple of Fortuna Virilis
late 2nd century	Temple of Hercules Victor

Monuments

800–300 B.C.	200–100 B.C.

Historical Events

Bronze funerary urn representing
a Villanovan hut

8th century	Etruscans in Italy		200–196	Second Macedonian war
753	Mythological founding of Rome		189	Victory over Antiochos III of Syria
650–510	Rome as Etruscan city		188	Occupation of Asia
534–509	Tarquinius Superbus, Etruscan king		172	Third Macedonian war
509	Etruscan monarchy driven from Rome		168	Victory over Perseus at Pydna
450	Code of Twelve Tables (*Lex duodecim tabularum*)		149–146	Third Punic war
390	Rome sacked by Gauls		146	Scipio Aemilianus destroys Carthage
343–298	Three Samnite wars		146	Mummius destroys Corinth
275	Roman victory over Pyrrhus		137–133	Siege of Numantia in Spain
272	Roman conquest of Tarento		125	Invasion of Gallia Transalpina
265	Roman occupation of Italy		120	Province of Gallia Narbonensis
264–241	First Punic war		113	Province of Asia
241	Occupation of Sicily		102	Marius conquers the Teutons
222	Occupation of Gallia Cisalpina			
219–202	Second Punic war (Hannibal)			
215–205	War against Philip V of Macedonia			
202	Roman victory at Zama			

Street lined with tombs at the
Etruscan burial site of Cerveteri

Arcades of the substructure supporting the Republican Temple of Terracina

Cavea of the Theater of Leptis Magna in Tripolitania (A.D. 1–2)

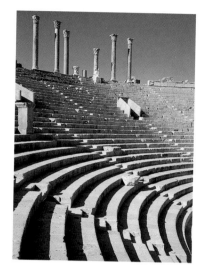

100	Cori: Temple of Hercules
80	Palestrina: Temple of Fortuna Primigenia
80–60	Tivoli: Temple of Hercules Victor
80–72	Tivoli: Temple of Sibyl or Vesta
80–25	Pompeii: second style
c. 80	Ostia: city walls
c.80	Terracina: Temple of Jupiter Anxur
55	Rome: Basilica Aemilia
from 54	Rome: Forum Julium

50	Rome: Theater of Pompey
48	Rome: Temple of Venus Genetrix
c. 45	Casinum: Varro's Aviary
from 42	Rome: Forum of Augustus
c. 40	Baiae: so-called Temple of Mercury
40–36	Rome: Domus Augustana
from 31	Rome: Temple of Mars Ultor
from 25	Pompeii: third style
23–11	Rome: Theater of Marcellus
19–13	Nimes: Pont du Gard
c.13	Arles: Cryptoporticuses
12	Nimes: Maison Carrée

1–2	Leptis Magna: Theater
14–37	Sperlonga: Grotto of Tiberius
18–25	Mérida: Theater
26	Orange: Triumphal Arch
28	Rome: Mausoleum of Augustus
44–54	Ostia: Port of Claudius

100–50 B.C.

50–1 B.C.

A.D. 1–50

100	War against pirates in Cilicia
91–87	Civil war
87	Marius triumphs in Rome
86	Sulla conquers Athens
82	Sulla establishes dictatorship
74–64	Third Mithridatic war
74–67	Provinces of Bithynia and Pontus
70	Consulate of Pompey and Crassus
61	Teutons invade Gaul
59	Consulate of Caesar
58–55	Caesar in Gaul and Germany
52	Consulate of Pompey

50	End of the Gallic war
49	Caesar crosses the Rubicon
48	Pompey assassinated in Egypt
44	Caesar assassinated on the Ides of March in Rome
43	Triumvirate of Octavian, Antonius, Lepidus
31	Octavian's victory at Actium
30	Egypt becomes a Roman province
30–25	Vitruvius, *De architectura*
27	Octavian granted honorary name of Augustus: principate
23	*Imperium majus* conferred on Augustus
12	Augustus becomes *pontifex maximus* (official head of Roman religion)
2	Regulations for imperial cult established

11	Campaigns in Germany
13	Tiberius co-emperor
14	Death of Augustus; Tiberius becomes emperor over 4,937,000 citizens
15	Sejanus commander of Praetorian Guard
27	Tiberius withdraws to Capri
30	*Imperium* conferred on Sejanus
34	Annexation of Judaea
37	Death of Tiberius, Caligula becomes emperor
41	Caligula assassinated, Claudius becomes emperor
43	Campaign in Britain
45	Annexation of Thrace
48–49	Corbulo in Germany

Wallpainting in the Villa dei Misteri in Pompeii (60 B.C.)

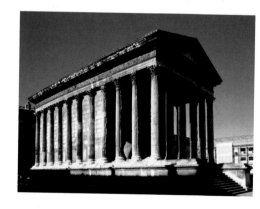

The Maison Carrée in Nimes, dedicated to the cult of Augustus and the imperial family

Wallpainting of a Pompeian house with decor in the form of a *scaenae frons* in the third or fourth style

Dome and *oculus* of the Pantheon built by Hadrian in Rome

52	Rome: Porta Maggiore
from 64	Rome: Domus Aurea of Nero
from 65	Pompeii: forum rebuilt
70–80	Rome: Colosseum
c. 70	Nimes: Amphitheater
71–75	Rome: Temple of Pax
80–92	Rome: Domus Flavia
82	Rome: Arch of Titus
96	Djemila: founded by Nerva
98	Rome: Forum of Nerva

100	Sabratha: Theater
c. 100	Baiae: so-called Temple of Diana
c. 100	Segovia: aqueduct
104	Rome: Baths of Trajan
107–112	Rome: Forum of Trajan
113	Rome: Trajan's Column
113	Ostia-Portus: Harbour of Trajan
113–114	Rome: Markets of Trajan

118–138	Tivoli: *Villa Hadriana*
121–137	Rome: Temple of Venus and Rome
from 121	Rome: Pantheon
124	Scotland: Hadrian's Wall
from 130	Rome: Hadrian's Mausoleum
c. 130	Zaghouan: Temple of the Waters
c. 130	Ostia: Horrea Epagathiana
138	Sbeitla: Forum
c.166	Dougga: Capitol
173	Rome: Triumphal Arch of Marcus Aurelius

A.D. 50–100

A.D. 100–120

A.D. 120–180

50	Claudius adopts Nero
54	Claudius assassinated, Nero becomes emperor
58	Corbulo's campaign in Armenia
63	Earthquake in Pompeii
64	Great fire of Rome
66–69	Jewish war of Vespasian
68	Death of Nero, Galba becomes emperor
69	Insurrection in Gaul; Rhine army revolts
69	Otho and Vitellius become emperors
70	Titus conquers and destroys Jerusalem
72	Annexation of Commagene
73	Conquest of Masada
77	Campaign in Germany
79	Pompeii: eruption of Vesuvius
79	Death of Vespasian, Titus emperor
80	Agricola in Scotland
81	Death of Titus, Domitian emperor
83	Conspiracy against Domitian
85–86	Campaigns agains the Dacians
90	Germanic provinces ruled by Domitian's terror
96	Domitian assassinated, Nerva emperor
98	Death of Nerva, Trajan emperor

100	Pliny the Younger is consul; *Letters*
101–102	First war against the Dacians
105	Second war against the Dacians
105–106	Conquest of Arabia
107	Annexation of Dacia
114	Campaign against the Parthians
116	Trajan in Mesopotamia
117	Death of Trajan in Cilicia, Hadrian becomes emperor
117	Hadrian evacuates Mesopotamia

Reconstruction of the interior of a library at the Forum of Trajan in Rome (after James E. Packer)

121–128	Hadrian's first journey
128–133	Hadrian's second journey
133	Jewish insurrection
135	Hadrian conquers Jerusalem
138	Adoption of Antoninus Pius
138	Death of Hadrian; Antoninus Pius emperor
140	*Imperium* conferred on Marcus Aurelius
161	War in Armenia against Vologaeses
161	Death of Antoninus Pius; Marcus Aurelius emperor; Verus co-emperor
163	Conquest of Artaxata
167–175	First Marcoman war
169	Death of Lucius Verus
178–180	Second Marcoman war

The Teatro Marittimo of the *Villa Hadriana* in Tivoli

180 Rome: Column of Marcus Aurelius
200–238 Thysdrus (El Djem): Amphitheater
203 Rome: Triumphal Arch of Septimius Severus
210–216 Leptis Magna: New Forum
212–216 Rome: Baths of Caracalla
c. 225 Dougga: Temple of Juno Caelestis

271–279 Rome: Aurelian Walls
early 4th century: Piazza Armerina: palace
298–306 Rome: Baths of Diocletian
305 Trier: Imperial Baths
306–312 Rome: Basilica of Maxentius and Constantine
310 Trier: Basilica (Aula Palatina)
315 Rome: Arch of Constantine

The Aurelian Walls, built to protect the city of Rome in the third century

The Severan amphitheater of El Djem (Tunisia)

The baths at Bath, indicating the romanization of England

Monuments

A.D. 180–230

A.D. 230–320

Historical Events

180 Death of Marcus Aurelius, Commodus becomes emperor
182–183 Conspiracies against the emperor
190 Commodus' reign of terror
192 Commodus assassinated
193 Year of Four Emperors: Septimius Severus, Pertinax, Clodius Albinus and Pescennius Niger struggle for power
193 Septimius Severus becomes emperor
197 Death of Albinus
197–202 War against the Parthians
197–202 Septimius Severus in the Orient
203 Septimius Severus in Africa
208–209 Death of Septimius Severus, Geta becomes emperor
211–217 Government of Caracalla
218–222 Government of Elgabal
222–235 Government of Severus Alexander

234 Alemanni at the Rhine
235 Maximianus Thrax becomes emperor
238–253 Power struggles and upheaval
244 Alemanni in Alsace and Rhaetia
245 Philippus fights in Dacia
249 Decius defeats the Goths and Vandals
252 Valerian appointed emperor
253 Alemanni and Franks in Gaul
261 Gallienus against the Barbarians
270 Aurelian becomes emperor
271–273 Aurelian defeats the Alemanni and conquers Palmyra
275–276 Aurelian assassinated, Probus becomes emperor
281 Usurpers in Gaul
282 Probus murdered, Carus becomes emperor
284 Diocletian becomes emperor
286 Diocletian and Maximian August
287–295 Renewal of empire
305 Abdication of Diocletian and Maximinian
306 Constantine is declared Augustus
307–324 Struggles between Maxentius, Licinius and Constantine

324 Constantine restores the unity of the empire (Byzantium as capital)
330 Constantinople becomes Christian imperial capital

The fourth century imperial basilica or Aula Palatina in Trier

GLOSSARY

Agora. Public square forming the administrative, religious, and commercial center of the Greek city.

Alveus. Pool or, more specifically, bath.

Apodyterium. Changing room in the public baths.

Apse. An inner area, either semi-circular or polygonal, opening on to a main nave. The apse plays the part of an *exedra*. It may feature at the ends of a basilica or in thermal rooms.

Aqueduct. A conduit or channel for water which may be underground or elevated above ground when it crosses low areas on bridges. The term has ended up being applied principally to the structures supporting the channel.

Arch. A curved construction over an opening. An arch is a structure formed by archstones, whose wedge-shaped voussoirs are radially jointed. Most Roman arches are round arches.

Arcade. An opening surmounted by an arch; an arcade may be a range of arches and openings, forming a portico.

Architrave. A lintel or frame resting on two vertical supports (columns or pillars). It is the horizontal part of the trilithon.

Arch-stone. A wedge-shaped architectural element which is part of an arch, vault or lintel. Synonymous with voussoir.

Area sacra. The sacred area, often confused with the *temenos*, the land consecrated to a god, the sacred enclosure of the temple.

Atrium. The central hall at the entrance of the Roman house with a central opening in the roof (the *compluvium*) and a pool below (the *impluvium*). Several rooms lead off this rectangular hall.

Aula regia. Throne room or audience chamber. Later synonymous with palace.

Barrel (or tunnel-vault). Describes a round vault of semi-circular form. The stone vault has arch-stones. The barrel vault may also be curved.

Basilica. Public market hall or court building. Originally a rectangular building with central nave flanked by aisles and an apse at the end. Later any large covered hall-like building.

Bond. The size and layout of stones or bricks in the wall.

Bucraneum. Portrayal of a bull's head or ox skull often found as a decorative element in a frieze.

Caldarium. Hall in the baths containing the hot pool; the steam room of a thermal establishment.

Cardo. The main street generally oriented north-south in the Roman urban system. It applied first to the Roman camp, then more generally to the creation of the checkerboard town layout.

Castrum. Roman military camp, generally square or rectangular in layout.

Cathisma. The imperial box in a circus or hippodrome.

Cavea. Auditorium of a theater, so called because originally it was excavated from a hillside.

Cella. The enclosed area of a temple where the statue of the divinity was kept, the *naos* of the temple.

Centuriation. The division of an area of land into regular lots earmarked for Roman settlers. It forms a squaring governed by the road axes, or which develops from the *cardo* and the *decumanus* of a city.

Ciborium. A small building in the form of a canopy supported by columns. It represented an honorific symbol placed over the throne of a ruler or over the statue of a god.

Cladding. A covering in sheets of stone (marble or travertine) affixed to the masonry of a construction.

Coenatio. Originally denoted a family dining room but came to refer to a ceremonial room, a reception room in a villa or a palace.

Columbarium. Underground burial chamber with rows of small recesses for the urns of ashes.

Column. A vertical, round, architectural support. It consists of a shaft, rests on a base, and is toped by a capital. As an aesthetic ensemble, the column expresses different ornamental styles.

Comitium. A place where the *comices* (legislative assembly) assembled; later denoted the assembly of the Roman people meeting in a circular area next to the Roman Forum.

Compluvium. Square opening in the roof of the *atrium*, forming the light source.

Concrete. An artifical material obtained by mixing gravel, ballast and brick debris with a mortar which forms the bond. When concrete hardens it forms a monolithic mass, widely used by the Romans in their architecture.

Corbelling (or cantilever). A construction technique for roofing obtained by a series of projecting courses which jut from the wall. Architecturally speaking, the corbelled vault is considered a false vault.

Course. Layer of dressed stones, or gap between two superposed layers forming a masonry wall.

Cryptoporticus. Vaulted underground corridor, often supporting the portico, with lighting through apertures in the vault.

Cubiculum. Bedroom, usually of small dimensions, in the Roman home.

Damnatio memoriae. Sentence pronounced by the Roman Senate condemning to oblivion the name of an emperor; a malediction on a ruler considered to be evil and whose actions are cursed.

Decastyle. A portico consisting of ten columns.

Decumanus. One of the two axes of the Roman camp (see *cardo*), then the main street running east-west crossing the *cardo* at the forum in a Roman town built on an orthogonal plan.

Dromos. Vaulted passage leading to a subterranean tomb.

Ecclesia. Assembly of citizens in the city.

Emblema. Part of a floor mosaic forming the center of the design; often created with finer fragments than the rest of the composition.

Emporium. Market, counter, commercial establishment; originally applied to the port of Rome situated on the left bank of the Tiber.

Entablature. The upper part of a classical building formed by the architrave, frieze, and cornice.

Euripe. Deriving from the canal separating the island of Euboea and Boeotia; the *euripe* became a moat or pool separating the two tracks of a hippodrome in the place of the *spina*. Also the canal that encircled the arena of the amphitheater to protect the spectators in the front row from the wild animals.

Exedra. A meeting place with seating; became a recess in an architectural structure, usually semicircular or sometimes rectangular. The *exedra* was often placed on the edge of a portico.

Formwork (or shuttering). Temporary wooden frames acting as moulds for casting concrete. Once the mortar has "gone off", the formwork is removed.

Framework. The triangular system of a timber frame. The framework (or truss roofing) is the ensemble of wooden roofs covering a building. Open-truss frame roofs are found in buildings where there are no ceilings.

Frigidarium. The cold room of a Roman bath.

Frons scaenae (or *scaenae frons*). The stage wall; the facade built opposite the *cavea* with its doors and stories of colonnades. The *frons scaenae* came to symbolize the city of the gods.

Hexastyle. A portico consisting of six columns.

Hypocauston. Underground furnace that provided heating for the thermal baths or rooms in a private dwelling.

Hypogeum. An underground room, vault or tomb.

Hypostyle. A hall whose roof is supported by rows of pillars or columns.

Impluvium. Pool placed in the center of the *atrium* receiving rain water from the opening of the *compluvium*.

Insula. Block or urban island; then, by extension, block on several floors of either apartments or administrative and commercial offices.

Intersection. The place where two barrel vaults meet to form a rib intersecting the two vaults.

Jus romanum. Roman law; the judicial system of ancient Rome.

Laconicum. The part of the *caldarium* in the thermal baths that formed the steam room.

Latifundia. The large agricultural estates; vast farms cultivated by slaves.

Limes. Defensive fortified line on the frontier of the Roman Empire.

Lintel. The horizontal element over an opening, window or door, which bears the load of the superstructure. It plays the same kind of role as the architrave.

Macellum. Market; initially of meat, then of fish and vegetables.

Mortar. Mixture of sand and lime used as a bond in masonry. Mortar is part of the composition of Roman concrete.

Naos. The hall of a temple containing the effigy of the deity; the holy of holies of the sanctuary.

Natatio. The swimming pool, generally in the open air, of the Roman baths.

Nymphaeum. A monumental fountain dedicated to the gods of water and springs (nymphs). The nymphaeum consists of basins, columns, canopies and statues, and ends up resembling the *frons scaenae* of theatres.

Oblong. Describes a space that is wider than it is deep, or a room of elongated breadth.

Octostyle. Describes a temple or building with eight columns on the façade.

Oculus. Circular aperture in a wall or roof.

Oikoumene. The entire world's population; the inhabited earth.

Orbis terrarum. The terrestrial globe — not to be confused with the *orbis coeli*, the celestial vault.

Pendentive. A spherical concave triangle forming the link at the corners of a building with a square plan with the circular base of a dome covering it.

Peripteral. Describes a building surrounded by colonnades on all sides.

Peristyle. A colonnade running all round a courtyard or square.

Pilaster. A slightly salient vertical pier in a wall. It has a base and a capital. It is akin to a lesene, which is surmounted by a frieze of small arches.

Pillar. A square, cross-shaped or polygonal vertical support.

Plastering. A layer of plaster or mortar applied to the facing of a wall. The plaster may be slightly sculpted or prepared to be painted on.

Platband. A straight lintel with arch-stone linking two supports. The platband works like an arch with arch-stones and bears the load of the superstructures.

Podium. The raised base of a Roman temple. This hight basement is accessible by one or more slights of stairs. This term is also applied to the basement of the *cavea* of a theater.

Portico. A colonnade forming a covered passage or a continuous gallery.

Pseudo-peripteros. Describes a temple whose façade columns are in relief, whereas those along the sides of the *cella* are not.

Quadriporticus. A series of four colonnades surrounding a space (garden, courtyard or square). The quadriporticus is a huge square peristyle.

Ribbed vault (or ribbing). A roofing system resulting from the intersection of two perpendicular round vaults, giving rise to diagonal ribs. This solution is commonly adopted in Roman vaulting.

Round arch. The term for an arch describing a semicircle.

Saddle-roof. Describes a wooden roof with two slopes.

Sanctum palatium. The sacred palace. The house of the deified sovereign was a religious place.

Scaenae frons. (see *frons scaenae*).

Spina. A longitudinal wall separating the two tracks of the hippodrome.

Squinch. A vaulted architectural element at the angle of a dome affording the transition from the square plan to the octagon and circle. It consists of a small cul-de-four angle vault. Not to be confused with the pendentive (cf.)

Stoa. Colonnaded walkway providing shelter, often at the edge of a public area such as an agora or forum.

Stucco. Architectural material for cladding and decoration consisting of fine plaster, casting lime and marble dust bonded together with a glue made of plant or animal extracts. Stucco may be coloured in the mix and can replicate marble. It is suitable for very refined relief works.

Synnaos. The figure who presides beside the effigy of the god in the *naos* of a temple. Applies to deified sovereigns who share the *cella* of the sanctuary with the god.

Tablinum. Room at the far end of the *atrium*, before the peristyle; an intermediary space of the Roman house that could be closed off into a reception room with movable wooden partitions or curtains.

Temenos. Area consecrated to a god; sacred area surrounding a temple.

Template. A wooden form or pattern used for the construction of an arch or vault.

Tepidarium. The warm rooms leading to the *caldarium* in the Roman baths.

Tesserae. Small pieces of marble, coloured stone or glass used for making mosaics.

Tetrastyle. Describes a temple or building with four columns on the façade.

Thermal baths. Public or private Roman baths consisting of a changing room *(apodyterium)*, cold bathroom *(frigidarium)*, warm bathroom *(tepidarium)*, hot bathroom *(caldarium)* with a steam bath or steamroom *(laconicum)* heated by hypocaust, as well as a swimming pool *(natatio)*.

Thermopolium. A public counter placed at the side of the street where one could buy drinks and snacks.

Tholos. Round temple with circular and concentric colonnades and *cella*.

Tribunalia. The emperor's box at the theater or basilica.

Triclinium. Room in a Roman house acting as a dining room and containing three couches disposed in a U shape around a small table. Originally denoting a bed containing three places. A ritual based on the sharing of food develops there.

Triconchos. Trefoil-shaped room.

Triglyph. A decorative part of the Doric frieze, consisting of two vertical grooves flanked by two half-grooves, forming a slightly salient motif, the rhythm of which alternates with the metopes.

Trilithon (or *trilith*). Architectural structure formed by two pillars and a lintel.

Vault. Arched roofing system, in dressed stone, brickwork or concrete, which, in Roman architecture, generally gives a barrel or semi-circular shape.

Velum. An awning of canvas stretched over the spectators in a theater or amphitheater to protect them from the sun.

Vicus. Village of huts, country farm, then road or district of a village.

Volumen. A roll of parchment forming a chapter or a book.

Voussoir. Synonymous with arch-stone or vault-stone.

Bibliography

In this selective bibliography on Roman architecture, the author not only lists the titles of major books and studies which act as general sources, but also includes works by specialists in comparative architecture, who contribute their own interpretation of the symbolic and semiological features of certain buildings. Lastly, he mentions various essays by specialists to which he has referred to develop his own hypotheses.

Adam, Jean-Pierre: *La construction romaine: matériaux et techniques.* Paris, 1989.

Alföldi, Andreas: *Die Ausgestaltung des monarchischen Zeremoniells am römischen Kaiserhofe,* Mitteilungen des deutschen archäologischen Instituts, Römische Abteilung, vol. 48. 1933.

Alföldi, Andreas: *Die Geschichte des Throntabernakels,* in: La Nouvelle Clio, 1–2. Brussels, 1949–1950.

Amy, Robert, et Pierre Gros: *La Maison Carrée de Nîmes,* 2 vol. Paris, 1979.

Andreae, Bernard: *L'Art de l'ancienne Rome.* Paris, 1973.

Andreae, Bernard: *Odysseus: Archäologie des europäischen Menschenbildes.* Frankfurt, 1982.

Andreae, Bernard et Baldassare Conticello: *Odysseus, Skylla und Charybdis.* Stuttgart, 1987.

Architecture et société – De l'archaïsme grec à la fin de la République romaine. Paris, 1982.

L'Art des peuples italiques. Naples, 1993.

Aurigemma, Salvatore: *Villa Adriana.* Rome, 1961.

Bammer, Anton: *Architektur und Gesellschaft in der Antike, Zur Deutung baulicher Symbole.* Vienne, 1985.

Baratte, François: *L'Art romain.* Paris, 1984.

Bauer, Heinrich: *Nuove ricerche sul Foro di Augusto,* in: L'Urbs, Espace urbain et Histoire. Rome, 1987.

Bauplanung und Bautheorie der Antike. Berlin, 1984.

Beaujeu, Jean: *La Vie scientifique à Rome au Ier siècle de l'Empire.* Paris, 1957.

Bianchi Bandinelli, Ranuccio: *Rome, the Centre of Power: Roman Art to A.D. 200.* London, 1970.

Bianchi Bandinelli, Ranuccio: *Rome, the Late Empire.* London, 1971.

Blake, Marion: *Roman Construction in Italy from Nerva through the Antonines.* Philadelphia, 1973.

Boëthius, Axel: *The Golden House of Nero – Some Aspects of Roman Architecture.* Ann Arbor, 1960.

Bon, A.: *La fontaine de Nîmes,* in: Mélanges Georges Radet, Revue des Etudes anciennes, XLII. Paris, 1940.

Bouché-Leclercq, Auguste: *Histoire de la divination dans l'Antiquité.* Paris, 1879–1882.

Bréhier, Louis: *Les institutions de l'Empire byzantin.* Paris, 1949.

Brilliant, Richard: *Roman Art from the Republic to Constantine.* London, 1974.

Brouquier-Reddé, Véronique: *Temples et cultes de Tripolitaine.* Paris, 1992.

Brown, F. E.: *Hadrianic Architecture,* in: Essays in Memory of Karl Lehmann. New York, 1964.

Buchner, Edmond: *Die Sonnenuhr des Augustus.* Mainz, 1982.

Caffarelli, Ernesto Vergara, et Giacomo Caputo: *Leptis Magna.* Verona, 1964.

Caputo, Giacomo: *Il Teatro di Sabratha e l'architettura teatrale africana.* Rome, 1959.

Carcopino, Jérôme: *Aspects mystiques du paganisme romain.* Paris, 1941.

Carcopino, Jérôme: *De Pythagore aux Apôtres.* Paris, 1956.

Carcopino, Jérôme: *Sylla ou la monarchie manquée.* Paris, 1931.

Carcopino, Jérôme: *La Vie quotidienne à Rome à l'apogée de l'Empire.* Paris, 1939.

Carettoni, Gianfilippo: *Das Haus des Augustus auf dem Palatin.* Mainz, 1983.

Cassius, Dion: *Histoire romaine.* Paris, 1867.

Chamoux, François: *La Civilisation hellénistique.* Paris, 1981.

Cicéron: *De la Divination.* Paris, 1837.

Coarelli, Filippo: *Architettura sacra e architettura privata nella tarda Repubblica,* in: Architecture et Société, colloque de 1980. Rome, 1983.

Coarelli, Filippo: *Guide archéologique de Rome.* Paris, 1994.

Crema, Luigi: *L'Architettura romana,* Enciclopedia classica. Turin, 1959.

Les Cryptoportiques dans l'Architecture romaine, Ecole française de Rome. 1973.

Cumont, Franz: *L'Iniziazione di Nerone da parte di Tiridate d'Armenia,* in: Revista di Filologia e d'Istruzione classica, XI. Turin, 1933.

Cunliffe, Barry: *Rome et son Empire,* Londres, 1978. Paris, 1994.

Etienne, Robert: *Pompéi, la cité ensevelie.* Paris, 1987.

Fasolo, F., et G. Gullini: *Il Santuario della Fortuna primigenia a Palestrina,* 2 vol. Rome, 1953.

Février, Paul-Albert: *L'art de l'Algérie antique.* Paris, 1971.

Fine Licht, Kjeld de: *The Rotunda in Rome – A Study of Hadrian's Pantheon.* Copenhagen, 1966.

Finsen, H.: *Domus Flavia sur le Palatin,* in: Analecta romanica, Suppl. 2. Frankfurt, 1962.

Finsen, H.: *La résidence de Domitien sur le Palatin,* in: Analecta romanica, Suppl. 5. Frankfurt, 1969.

Förtsch: *Archäologischer Kommentar zu den Villenbriefen des Jüngeren Plinius.* Mainz, 1993.

Frontin: *Les Aqueducs de la ville de Rome.* Paris, 1961.

Grenade, Pierre: *L'idéologie de l'Empire romain.* Paris, 1974.

Grimal, Pierre : *La Civilisation romaine.* Paris, 1960.

Grimal, Pierre : *Les Jardins romains.* Paris, 1984.

Grimal, Pierre : *Pompéi – Demeures secrètes.* Paris, 1992.

Gros, Pierre: *Aurea Templa: recherches sur l'architecture religieuse à Rome à l'époque d'Auguste.* Paris, 1976.

Gros, Pierre: *Architecture et société à Rome et en Italie centro-méridionale aux deux derniers siècles de la République.* Brussels, 1978.

Gros, Pierre: *La Fonction symbolique des édifices théâtraux,* in: L'Urbs, espace urbain et histoire. Rome, Paris, 1987.

Gros, Pierre: *Le projet Vitruve,* Indroduction au Colloque organisé par l'Ecole française de Rome en mars 1993. Rome, 1994.

Gros, Pierre: *Le schéma vitruvien du théâtre latin et sa signification dans le système normatif du de Architectura,* in: Rev. Arch. I/1994.

Gros, Pierre, et Mario Torelli: *Storia dell'urbanistica, Il mondo romano.* Rome-Bari, 1988.

Hampe, Roland: *Sperlonga und Vergil.* Mainz, 1972.

Haselberger, Lothar: *Antike Bauzeichnung des Pantheon entdeckt,* in: Antike Welt. Mainz, 4/1994.

Hermansen, Gustav: *Ostia, Aspects of Roman City Life.* Edmonton, 1982.

Herzfeld, Ernst: *Der Thron des Khosro,* in: Jahrbuch der preussischen Kunstsammlungen, vol. 41. Berlin, 1920.

Hoffmann, Adolf: *Das Gartenstadion in der Villa Hadriana.* Mainz, 1980.

Iacopi, Giulio: *L'Antro di Tiberio a Sperlonga.* Rome, 1963.

Kähler, Heinz: *Hadrian und seine Villa bei Tivoli.* Berlin, 1950.

Kähler, Heinz: *Das Fortuna Heiligtum von Palestrina,* Annales Universitatis Saraviensis. Saarbrücken, 1958.

Kähler, Heinz: *Rom und sein Imperium.* Baden-Baden, 1962.

Kähler, Heinz: *Der römische Tempel, Raum und Landschaft.* Berlin, 1970.

Kaiser Augustus und die verlorene Republik, Catalogue de l'Exposition. Berlin, 1988.

Kantorowicz, Ernst H.: *Laus Regiae: A Study in Liturgical Acclamations and Mediaeval Ruler Worship.* Berkeley, 1946.

Kantorowicz, Ernst H.: *Les deux Corps du Roi.* Paris, 1989.

Krause, Clemens, et alii: *Domus Tiberiana, Nuove Ricerche.* Zurich, 1985.

La Laurentine et l'invention de la Villa romaine. Paris, 1982.

Lassalle, Victor: *La Fontaine de Nîmes de l'Antiquité à nos jours.* Paris, 1967.

Lauter, Hans: *Die Architektur des Hellenismus.* Darmstadt, 1986.

Lavin, Irving: *The House of the Lord: aspects of the palace triclinia in the architecture of late antiquity and in the early Middle Ages,* in: Art Bulletin, XLIV. New York, 1962.

Lehmann, Karl: *The Dome of Heaven,* in: Art Bulletin, 27. New York, 1945.

Lézine, Alexandre: *Architecture romaine d'Afrique.* Paris, 1964.

MacDonald, William L.: *The Pantheon, Design, Meaning and Progeny.* Cambridge (Mass.), 1976.

MacDonald, William L.: *The Architecture of the Roman Empire.* New Haven, 1982.

Mau, August: *Geschichte der decorativen Wandmalerei in Pompeji.* Berlin, 1882.

Naumann, Rudolf: *Der Quellbezirk von Nîmes.* Berlin, 1937.

Niccolini, A.: *Arte Pompeiana.* Naples, 1887.

Nicolet, Claude: *Rome à la conquête du monde méditerranéen, 1. Les structures de l'Italie romaine.* Paris, 1979.

Nicolet, Claude: *id. 2. Genèse d'un empire.* Paris, 1978.

Orange, Hans Peter L': *Domus aurea – der Sonnenpalast,* in: Serta Eitremiana, 1, 1942.

Orange, Hans Peter L': *Studies on the Iconography of Cosmic Kingship in the Ancient World.* Oslo, 1953.

Orange, Hans Peter L': *L'Empire romain du IIIe au VIe siècle.* Milan, 1985.

La Peinture de Pompéi, Préface de Georges Vallet, textes de Karl Schefold *et alii,* 2 vol. Paris, 1993.

Petit, Paul: *La Paix romaine.* Paris, 1967.

Petit, Paul: *Histoire générale de l'Empire romain, 1. Le Haut-Empire.* Paris, 1974.

Petit, Paul: *id. 2. La Crise de l'Empire.* Paris, 1974.

Petit, Paul: *id. 3. Le Bas-Empire.* Paris, 1974.

Picard, Gilbert: *Empire romain.* Freiburg, 1965.

Pline le Jeune: *Lettres,* 3 vol. Paris, 1927–1928.

Pompei, Pitture e Mosaici, Enciclopedia Italiana, 4 vol. Rome, 1990–1991.

Pompéi – Travaux et envois des architectes français au XIXe siècle. Paris, 1981.

Price, Derek de Sola: *Gears from the Greeks, The Antikythera Mechanism, A Calendar Computer.* Philadelphia, 1974.

Prückner, Helmut et Sebastian Storz: *Beobachtungen im Oktogon der Domus Aurea,* in: Mitteilungen des deutschen archäologischen Instituts, Römische Abteilung, 81, 1974.

Rakob, Friedrich Ludwig: *Die Piazza d'Oro in der Villa Hadriana bei Tivoli.* Karlsruhe, 1970.

Rakob, Friedrich Ludwig: *"Römische Architektur",* in: Propyläen Kunstgeschichte. Berlin 1967.

Rémondon, Roger: *La Crise de l'Empire romain.* Paris, 1980.

Sauron, Gilles: *Le complexe pompéien du Champ de Mars, Nouveauté urbanistique à finalité idéologique,* in: L'Urbs, espace urbain et histoire. Rome, Paris, 1987.

Sauter, Franz: *Der römische Kaiserkult bei Martial und Statius.* Stuttgart, 1934.

Schefold, Karl: *La peinture pompéienne, Essai sur l'évolution de sa signification.* Brussels, 1972.

Schoppa, Helmut: *L'art romain dans les Gaules, en Germanie et dans les îles Britanniques.* Freiburg, s.d.

Scott, K.: *The imperial Cult under the Flavians.* Stuttgart, 1936.

Smith, E.B.: *Architectural Symbolism of imperial Rome and the Middle Ages.* Princeton, 1956.

Stierlin, Henri: *Hadrien et l'architecture romaine.* Paris, 1984.

Stierlin, Henri: *L'Astrologie et le Pouvoir, De Platon à Newton,* Préface de Pierre Grimal. Paris, 1986.

Stierlin, Henri: *L'Orient byzantin, De Constantinople à l'Arménie et de Syrie en Ethiopie.* Paris, 1988.

Stierlin, Henri: *Le développement de la mécanique antique sous l'impulsion de l'Astrologie,* in: Publications de l'Observatoire astronomique de Strasbourg, Série "Astronomie et Science humaines", Nº 8, 1993.

Swoboda, Karl M.: *Römische und Romanische Paläste.* Vienna, 1969.

Üblacker, Mathias: *Das Teatro Marittimo in der Villa Hadriana.* Mainz, 1985.

Urbs (L') Espace urbain et Histoire (Ier siècle avant J.-C. – IIIer siècle après J.-C.), Ecole française de Rome. Paris, 1987.

Varro, Terentius: *De re rustica, Venice 1965.*

Vighi, Roberto: *Villa Adriana.* Rome, 1958.

Vitruvius: *Pollio: De architectura libri decem.* Darmstadt, 1964.

Vitruve: *De l'architecture,* Livre IX. Paris, 1969.

Voisin, Jean-Louis: *Exoriente Sole (Suétone, Ner. 6). D'Alexandrie à la Domus Aurea,* in: L'Urbs, Espace urbain et Histoire. Rome, Paris, 1987.

Ward-Perkins, John B.: *Roman Architecture.* New York, 1977.

Warden, P. Gregory: *The Domus Aurea reconsidered,* in: Journal of the Society of Architectural Historians, XL, 4, December 1981.

Wataghin-Cantino, Gisella: *La Domus Augustana, Personalità e Problemi dell'Architettura Flavia.* Turin, 1966.

Wheeler, Mortimer (Sir): *Les influences romaines au-delà des frontières impériales.* Paris, 1960.

Zander, G.: *Nuovi Studi e ricerche sulla Domus Aurea,* in: Palladio, 15. Rome, 1965.

Zanker, Paul: *Augustus und die Macht der Bilder.* Munich, 1987.

Index–Monuments

Index–Persons

ACKNOWLEDGEMENTS AND CREDITS

The author and photographer wish to thank the Swiss Institute in Rome, and in particular: Dr Florens Deuchler, director, and Ms Verena Nucifora-Scheurer, secretary, for their assistance in obtaining the necessary photography permits for Italian sites and museums.

The publisher and the author are especially grateful to the following institutions: the Soprintendenza alle Antichità di Roma e di Napoli; the directorate of the Museo Nazionale Romano in Rome; the directorate of the Museo Capitolino in Rome; the directorate of the Museo Nazionale di Villa Giulia in Rome; the directorate of the Museo Nazionale in Naples; the directorate of the Museo in Albano.

Special thanks also to the Tunisian National Office for the Development and Protection of the Archeological and Historical Heritage for their kind assistance at the Musée National du Bardo in Tunis and the Musées Archéologiques in Sousse and El Djem.

The reconstructed wallpaintings of Pompeii on pages 116–117 are from the publication "Depinti murali di Pompei" by Edoardo Cerillo, Naples (19th century), which the Bibliothèque d'Art et d'Archéologie in Geneva kindly made available to the author.

For the photographs not taken by Anne and Henri Stierlin, Benedikt Taschen Verlag wishes to thank:
Page 99: © Callet/École Nationale Supérieure des Beaux-Arts.
Pages 104/105: © Chifflot/École Nationale Supérieure des Beaux-Arts.
Page 11: © André Corboz.
Pages 91, 152 top, 222 top left: © Robert P. Estall/Artephot.
Pages 3, 32 bottom: © Fototeca Unione at the American Academy in Rome.
Page 131: © Gilbert Gorski.
Pages 176/177: © Drawing Antonio Molino/Airone n. 99 7/89.
Pages 132/133: © James Packer.
Pages 216 bottom, 217 top, 223 top: © Josef Tietzen.
Page 217 bottom: © Yaph.
We extend our special thanks to Alberto Berengo Gardin for preparing the plans on pages 9, 21, 29, 32, 36, 42, 48, 54, 59, 60, 63, 71, 77, 79, 80, 85, 106, 108, 112, 118, 130, 136, 137, 139, 140, 154, 158, 160, 164, 166, 168, 178, 180, 186, 188, 190, 201, 204, 205, 207, 216, 219, 220, 221, 222, 223, 224, 225, 229.